CW01560581

Bitcoin & B

Technology Explained For

Beginners

How Bitcoin (BTC), Cryptocurrency (+ Altcoins) & The Blockchain Works & Why They Will Revolutionize Everyone's Life.

By Brian Scott Fitzgerald

Published By Fitzgerald Publishing Group

© Copyright Fitzgerald Publishing Group 2023 - All rights reserved.

The content contained within this book may not be reproduced, duplicated, or transmitted without direct written permission from the author or the publisher.

Under no circumstances will any blame or legal responsibility be held against the publisher, or author, for any damages, reparation, or monetary loss due to the information contained within this book. Either directly or indirectly. You are responsible for your own choices, actions, and results.

Legal Notice:

This book is copyright protected. This book is only for personal use. You cannot amend, distribute, sell, use, quote, or paraphrase any part of this book's content without the author's or publisher's consent.

Disclaimer Notice:

Please note that the information contained within this document is for educational and entertainment purposes only. All effort has been executed to present accurate, up-to-date, and reliable, complete information. No warranties of any kind are declared or implied. Readers acknowledge that the author does not render legal, financial, medical, or professional advice. The content within this book has been derived from various sources. Please consult a licensed professional before attempting any techniques outlined in this book.

By reading this document, the reader agrees that under no circumstances is the author responsible for any losses, direct or indirect, which are incurred as a result of the use of the information contained within this document, including, but not limited to, — errors, omissions, or inaccuracies.

Your Free Gift. I am offering my readers the FREE PDF version of ChatGPT Prompts. To get almost instant access, go to this website.. https://go.fitzgeraldpublishing.com/opt-in-page-crypto2. Or use your phone to take a picture of this QR code, and it will take you to the Website for your Gift.

Inside the book, you will discover:

- **3000 Prompts** To help you make even more money online.
- **Save time:** You can search for new topics to create content on ChatGPT.
- **Expand knowledge:** Our Package of ChatGPT Prompts covers various topics, from science and technology to art and culture.

If you want to make even more money online, grab this free PDF.

Wait, that's not all; just for buying this book and getting the free PDF above, you can also earn another free Book. You can use your phone to take a picture of this QR code.

Or go direct to the book page on Amazon at https://mybook.to/beyondchatgpt. Use the latest AI techniques to uncover online innovation's future. Take advantage! "Beyond ChatGPT and 50 New AI Tools: The Ultimate Guide to Discovering Cutting-Edge AI Tools Beyond ChatGPT" offers endless possibilities. Explore a variety of cutting-edge AI solutions to transform your work. Discover advanced AI tools beyond ChatGPT on this thrilling voyage. If you want to make even more money online, grab this free book.

How to Make Money Online: THE SERIES

I created a series of 12 (twelve) books, all Titled... How to Make Money with......

The series starts with the other Crypto book that goes with the one you are reading now...

Titled: How to Make Money Online with Crypto: Mastering Cryptocurrency, Bitcoin, Blockchain, NFTs, DeFi, Altcoins, and Other Digital Assets.

And then continue with the others......

How to Make Money Online with ChatGPT

How to Make Money Online with Social Media Marketing

How to Make Money Online with YouTube

How to Make Money Online with Blogging

How to Make Money Online with SEO

How to Make Money Online with Instagram

How to Make Money Online with TiK Tok

How to Make Money Online with Real Estate

How to Make Money Online with Stock Market

How to Make Money Online with Drop Shipping

How to Make Money Online with Affiliate Marketing

How to Make Money Online with Kindle Publishing

Feel free to read any of my books in the series, which can be found on my Author page on Amazon at https://www.amazon.com/author/brianscottfitzgerald.

Table of Contents

Introduction

Imagine a world where money isn't carried around in a wallet. Imagine a world where you can buy and sell things with just a simple tap of a button. Imagine a world where you never have to visit a bank or any other mainstream, traditional financial institution.

Now imagine a world where this new money-making system affects more than just how you spend and save. Imagine that this new world also alters how politics work, how people and customers are treated, and how poor citizens are treated. Imagine a world where money is wholly changed but acts as a domino and soon transforms everything associated with and tied to it.

It might sound like something out of a novel or the pipe dreams of someone who is all too hopeful about the future of our world. But a world like this can exist. We are *this* close to a world like this being the one we live in. We are on the verge of living in a society where we make, save, and spend money differently. While the changes could seem minor to some, they are massive and consequential.

We are also on the verge of a society where the status quo is radically shaken and changed - for the better. For generations, the people who have been considered at the bottom of the totem pole have yet to be treated as well as those at the top. It has resulted in a massive financial disparity between classes and a world where things are unfair. This system favored the rich, who only got richer, over the poor, who stayed poorer. But this newly proposed finance system can do away with a lot of that and create a level playing field. It can genuinely help lift people and keep things even and fair.

Again, these ideas are plausible. They are more than possible. To some, they are actually in development, in the works, and coming soon. Many people think that changing how money is made and spent won't have such a profound effect, but they are wrong. A change that is as seemingly simple as that really can set off a chain reaction that radically transforms the world around us. Not only is it possible, but it's also likely.

What will be the catalyst that does all of this? What is this major missing puzzle piece that has the power to alter the world as we know it? How can it do this? Who is in charge of it? What powers it?

The answer is you. This new financial system's power to revolutionize industries, businesses, and people is in your hands. That's because the key to unlocking all of this is cryptocurrency.

And the key to powering cryptocurrency is blockchain. And both cryptocurrency and blockchain are powered by, maintained by, and used by the people. It's not at the whim of major financial institutions like banks, mortgage lenders, and brokerage firms. No, it's used by the people who will benefit from it: regular citizens looking to get in the game and help make it fairer for everyone.

It's very accurate that cryptocurrency and blockchain technologies can change the world. Why is that true? Because it's already happening. You may not know it, but blockchain and crypto are already transforming how things are done, both big and small. You might not have noticed it, but it's very accurate. All over the world and throughout countless businesses, these two powerful electronic tools of the future are becoming benefits of the present and shaking things up.

Once you understand cryptocurrency and its blockchain engine, you will see how impressive it is. You will also know why investing in, believing in, and using it is so intelligent. You will see that cryptocurrency is about more than just buying and selling products. It's also about way more than trading crypto, like people trade commodities on Wall Street. No, cryptocurrency is about so, so much more than that. It's the largest, most powerful, and possibly most consequential silent protest in the history of the world.

You will also see that blockchain is about so much more than millions of people worldwide "mining" coins to make money off of them. Blockchain is about more than just powering various cryptocurrencies. No, blockchain is about helping businesses and entire massive industries perform better, faster, and safer. Blockchain is about updating and enhancing systems that have been stuck in time and outdated without even knowing it.

You will hear the terms cryptocurrency and blockchain used together often. To some, they are interchangeable. That's because they are so closely linked; they do work hand-in-hand. The truth is that one doesn't exist without the other. But while they are still very majorly linked and used together in all they do, they are also separated and working in great, impressive ways. Both cryptocurrency and blockchain are doing their things and branching out into other parts of the world, no longer forced to walk hand-in-hand across the globe. Seeing how they evolve and grow is fantastic, exciting, and impressive. And it's exciting to know that the sky is the limit for both of them.

It's no exaggeration to say that blockchain and cryptocurrency can change the world - and your life. They really can, and, in some ways, they already are. But you must truly understand how they work before you can comprehend what they have in store for you. You need to know what they are doing, why they are doing it, and *how* they are doing it before you can see the impact that will have on you.

Once you understand all those things, you will see how cryptocurrency and blockchain can help you and revolutionize your life in some radical ways. You can use it to your advantage for investing, spending, saving, and navigating a brand-new financial landscape that is making millions of dollars and improving businesses worldwide.

First, you need to know what cryptocurrency is. More importantly, you need to understand why it came to be. There is a deep, rich history of cryptocurrency and blockchain, even though both are only a bit over a decade old. Let's return to where it all started and find out how it began. More importantly, let's find out *why* it started.

What will be the catalyst that does all of this? What is this major missing puzzle piece that has the power to alter the world as we know it? How can it do this? Who is in charge of it? What powers it?

The answer is you. This new financial system's power to revolutionize industries, businesses, and people is in your hands. That's because the key to unlocking all of this is cryptocurrency. And the key to powering cryptocurrency is blockchain. And both cryptocurrency and blockchain are powered by, maintained by, and used by the people. It's not at the whim of major financial institutions like banks, mortgage lenders, and brokerage firms. No, it's used by the people who will benefit from it: regular citizens looking to get in the game and help make it fairer for everyone.

It's very accurate that cryptocurrency and blockchain technologies can change the world. Why is that true? Because it's already happening. You may not know it, but blockchain and crypto are already transforming how things are done, both big and small. You might not have noticed it, but it's very accurate. All over the world and throughout countless businesses, these two powerful electronic tools of the future are becoming benefits of the present and shaking things up.

Once you understand cryptocurrency and the blockchain engine behind it, you will see just how impressive it is. You will also know why investing in, believing in, and using it is so intelligent. You will see that cryptocurrency is about more than just buying and selling products. It's also about way more than trading crypto, like people trade commodities on Wall Street. No, cryptocurrency is about so, so much more than that. It's the largest, most powerful, and possibly most consequential silent protest in the history of the world.

You will also see that blockchain is about so much more than millions of people worldwide "mining" coins to make money off of them. Blockchain is about more than just powering various cryptocurrencies. No, blockchain is about helping businesses and entire massive industries perform better, faster, and safer. Blockchain is about updating and enhancing systems that have been stuck in time and outdated without even knowing it.

You will hear the terms cryptocurrency and blockchain used together often. To some, they are interchangeable. That's because they are so closely linked; they do work hand-in-hand. The truth is that one doesn't exist without the other. But while they are still very majorly linked and used together in all they do, they are also separated and working in great, impressive ways. Both cryptocurrency and blockchain are doing their things and branching out into other parts of the world, no longer forced to walk hand-in-hand across the globe. Seeing how they evolve and grow is fantastic, exciting, and impressive. And it's exciting to know that the sky is the limit for both of them.

It's no exaggeration to say that blockchain and cryptocurrency can change the world - and your life. They really can, and, in some ways, they already are. But you must truly understand how they work before you can comprehend what they have in store for you. You need to know what they are doing, why they are doing it, and *how* they are doing it before you can see the impact that will have on you.

Once you understand all those things, you will see how cryptocurrency and blockchain can help you and revolutionize your life in some radical ways. You can use it to your advantage for investing, spending, saving, and navigating a brand-new financial landscape that is making millions of dollars and improving businesses worldwide.

First, you need to know what cryptocurrency is. More importantly, you need to understand why it came to be. There is a deep, rich history of cryptocurrency and blockchain, even though both are only a bit over a decade old. Let's return to where it all started and find out how it began. More importantly, let's find out *why* it started.

What is Bitcoin

I don't know what level of experience you have with cryptocurrency or Bitcoin, but maybe we should start this book and end this introduction with a definition of what Bitcoin is…

Bitcoin is the first limited resource that can be confirmed entirely digitally.

Discover the cryptocurrency world with Bitcoin, the digital currency that utilizes cryptography to ensure top-notch security. Experience the convenience of a purely digital currency with bitcoins. Unlike traditional currencies, bitcoins have no physical form. Instead, they are represented by balances associated with public and private keys, which can be explained as long numbers and letters linked through a sophisticated mathematical encryption algorithm.

The "limited resource" that is Bitcoin has captured the attention of investors and technologically savvy people worldwide. With a hard cap of 21 million bitcoins, the potential for scarcity has driven demand to new heights. Satoshi Nakamoto, the brilliant mind behind Bitcoin, embedded this restriction into the code. Mining new Bitcoins is becoming increasingly challenging and resource-intensive due to the growing number of mined bitcoins. Similarly, Bitcoin's behavior resembles a scarce commodity, like gold and silver.

Discover the seamless process of verifying transactions on the Bitcoin Blockchain, where confirmation is achieved entirely through digital means. Experience the secure and transparent world of Bitcoin transactions. The Network of "miners" tirelessly verifies each transaction through complex mathematical problem-solving. Once verified, the transaction is added to the unalterable Bitcoin blockchain, ensuring security and transparency.

Mining is a fully digital process that enables the Bitcoin network to confirm transactions and prevent duplicate spending without needing a trusted third party. Mining is also the term for the method through which Bitcoins are created. Bitcoin is an unprecedented development since it is an entirely digital, finite resource that utilizes a decentralized verification system.

Chapter 1: Cryptocurrency 101 - What is It?

What, how, where, when, and why? You have indeed been told in the past that those are the most important questions to ask when you are trying to figure something out and wrap your head around it and truly understand it. Those are the basic building blocks to genuinely comprehending a subject or event. With those, you will be aware of something.

That is true for cryptocurrency, which has proven very complicated for millions. Just the word alone is enough to scare people away and not entice them to learn more. Scores and scores of people think cryptocurrency is a super-advanced, complex, intimidating system that is too tricky to wrap their heads around. While cryptocurrency is very deep and its strategy is difficult, nothing should scare anyone. Cryptocurrency is simple when you break it down, especially when examining its principles, beliefs, and concepts.

Who? What? Where? When and why? Much of that information about cryptocurrency will reveal itself as we tell its tale, but it is best to start by asking why—the why is so valuable when it comes to cryptocurrency. Unlike many other markets ' assets, cryptocurrency wasn't created simply so people could make millions of dollars. Initially, cryptocurrency was a way for protesters to speak out. Those in power were being sent a message. The importance of this cannot be overstated. One of the reasons cryptocurrency started - and still does - was the power of its meaning and message. Many people believe in cryptocurrency because it is not just about making money. What it stands for, what it represents, is what they believe in.

Those who created cryptocurrency and championed it from the beginning are unique investors, as you will see when studying cryptocurrency. Their goal is to make a point and have a voice. A message is being sent, and a system is being changed. Making money is one of many goals. In truth, these people started Bitcoin and cryptocurrency for a righteous cause and belief.

Many of these invigorated and committed traders are still involved in the crypto market to this day, which is why it's so crucial that you understand why they made the decisions they did. Since the marketplace they crafted was created in their image, you will be better able to understand them. You can better navigate cryptocurrency once you know what the pioneers thought. Perhaps you even hold the same principles they do.

What is Cryptocurrency?

Here is the million-dollar question that confuses many, even though it is simple and the answer is plain. As easy as it is, you need to master it before you can master anything else, especially since so many people still ask for it even as cryptocurrency takes hold and becomes more and more successful.

So, here is the question that consumes and confuses so many: what is cryptocurrency? How many people have asked that? And how many have been able actually to answer accurately?

It's a digital currency. Doesn't that seem straightforward? Crypto has so much more to offer than that, but that's the main point. Unlike conventional currencies, such as debit cards, credit cards, or cash in your wallet, all cryptocurrencies are digital money that can be spent to buy goods and services. Cryptocurrency can be used to buy anything, despite what some might think. Certain places allow you to purchase plane tickets, home furnishing, food, and even cars with cryptocurrency. When you think of what cryptocurrency can do, look at it as no different from the Dollar, Yen, or any other form of payment you see worldwide.

What sets cryptocurrency apart is two things: how it is held and how it is kept safe. Those are two radically different approaches to money and two of the main reasons why people don't understand it or, worse yet, fear it. When you hear people talk about cryptocurrency, many will talk about its safety. Millions think that cryptocurrency isn't safe, but that's because they don't know how it works. If they were to learn the truth, like you will, they would see that cryptocurrency is far safer than almost any other currency in the world.

But aside from the safety, a prominent attractive selling point about crypto is its nature and how it is stored. This crypto area confuses you; you can't blame people for being in the dark about it. It's a valid question: how do you physically keep your hands on Bitcoin or cryptocurrency? But you don't. Unlike traditional forms of currency, you will never have a Bitcoin in your hands or your wallet. You will never hold cryptocurrency. It does not exist that way. It is purely digital, only living online in every way. For many, that needs to be clarified, something they cannot wrap their heads around. If there is value in cryptocurrency - and there is - how can you not keep it with you and keep it safe that way? How do you pay for goods and services with an item you cannot physically hand over to someone? How does that make any sense? How is their value in things that you cannot see?

But there is value in your credit card transactions. The same is true with your debit card transactions too. When you write a check, no one questions the value of your review. Therefore, when you think about it, it makes sense that cryptocurrency can hold plenty of weight without ever being something you have in your hands. Still, many people need help getting into the idea of cryptocurrency because it will never be something they fold into their wallets or hand to a cashier.

The other radical and different thing about cryptocurrency is how it is kept safe. That is what brings us to the concept of blockchain. Blockchain is a massive, ever-changing online ledger system supporting every cryptocurrency transaction in check. Spread across computers worldwide, the blockchain is a living and breathing thing, a gigantic code that keeps every transaction visible and accountable. It is a wildly different way of keeping track of the world of cryptocurrency, and we will get into it much more later. But rest assured that no matter how complicated and different blockchain is, it is also one of cryptocurrency's most critical and revolutionary aspects and makes it safe and secure.

Far too many people view cryptocurrency as fake money, as something that isn't real and shouldn't be looked at in the same ways as traditional currencies. But that is such a short-sighted way to view it. Is cryptocurrency different? Yes. Does it still have much room to grow before it is as powerful as the dollar? Yes. But does it have just as much potential and promise as any other currency? It sure does. Even though something is new and radically different, it must still be more critical than its peers.

There was a time when the television seemed radical, as did the airplane, the internet, and more.

Right now, millions still view cryptocurrency as a bizarre little currency that only a select few people use online. That is wildly inaccurate. Not only do millions of people worldwide invest in and use cryptocurrency, but it is now minor. It has grown so much over the last decade. If people knew how it started and how little value it once had, they would no longer call cryptocurrency little.

Why Cryptocurrency?

Why should I use cryptocurrency? You will hear that question again and again. Even you might be asking yourself. Why should I even read about it, learn about it, or give it a second thought? Why not use the forms of money I am used to, the traditional currencies I have known all my life? Why risk cryptocurrency when I already have it so good with what I have?

These are valid questions and ones that many people will ask. The answer is different for everyone, and there are many legitimate and proper reasons why people dive into crypto. However, the typical response is that cryptocurrency holds more potential, promise, and power than any other form of currency worldwide. It also has value in more ways than one, making it attractive to both people looking to perfect their approach to wealth management and people looking to invest.

Some people buy into cryptocurrency because they believe in its cause and what it stands for. That is why so many people jumped into the crypto world when it first launched. It was a form of protest, saying something and taking a stand. Other people use cryptocurrency because they think it has the chance to be the future currency. They see when people can walk into their corner store and pay with their crypto wallet instead of traditional money. Then others invest in crypto because they want to ride the market and make a profit. Like the stock market, some people buy into cryptocurrency to ride the market's wave, cash out at the right time, and walk away with more money than when they started. It's a wise investment, as made evident by the millions of people who have made lots of money off it.

For these reasons, modern cryptocurrencies should be considered a currency and a commodity. That means it is something you can spend, like cash, and invest and trade in. Essentially if you own any cryptocurrency, you are holding stock in that crypto. The market that it's a part of has proven, again and again, that it can create significant gains for those involved. Unlike so many other assets and industries, there are so many reasons why people should get into cryptocurrency. There is more than one solid, definitive reason but dozens and dozens. Each is valid, can stand independently, and is enough to sway even the most cautious and uncertain investor. Cryptocurrency has many different possible uses and so many attractive features, and so many exciting aspects that the reasons why are countless and seemingly constantly growing.

The truth is that investing in *anything* is a risk. Investing in something as common and useful as milk could still be risky because you cannot control the world around you or prevent other investors or the market. If you are looking for something risk-free, investing in crypto - or anything - isn't for you.

But beginning a cryptocurrency journey isn't about abandoning traditional money. It is about expanding your abilities and financial horizons. It is about being ahead of the curve and realizing that industries can and will change. The future will catch up with us; it always has. There have been many examples of something we thought was steadfast and eternal changing. People never thought anyone would see a motion picture because the radio was the preferred method of entertainment. Then theaters became a massive entertainment enterprise. Then people thought that no one would stream movies from home because they preferred theaters, and using so much bandwidth was unreliable and expensive. Now entire movie studios pour their films at home before they even hit theaters. This is just one example of how times change. Accepting and understanding cryptocurrency is about your desire to be a part of what is ahead. It isn't about abandoning or getting rid of traditional currencies.

It's about saying there can be more options for everyone - and you want a part of that.

You certainly have to be careful when you begin using cryptocurrency. Just like physical money, it can evaporate when careless and reckless. But using it successfully and smartly can lead to expanding your wealth tenfold. It can also ween you off the traditional banking methods and schemes that have helped and hurt many more.

Cryptocurrencies exist solely in a safe digital environment thanks to cutting-edge technology. Your finances will stay secure and off-limits to unruly hackers, greedy governments, and money-hungry banks. Thanks to robust and reliable encryption, fraud and interference are not a part of the cryptocurrency system. Cryptocurrency provides a safe, anonymous, and completely personalized financial system that is modern and completely digital. It feels like the future wave because it *is* the coming wave.

Cryptocurrency and blockchain have existed for over ten years, still shrouded in mystery and confusion. Even those who think they know it best really do not. And those who know little are fed misinformation or false facts. This book seeks to change so everyone, from a new investor to an old pro, understands Bitcoin and how it can change the world.

Does Cryptocurrency Have Potential?

Cryptocurrency causes more confusion than any other word in the modern age. People hear and see the word constantly, in the media and even among friends and family. Yet, nearly every time it is mentioned, it is met with multiple questions and utter suspicion. Even as cryptocurrency has become more popular over the years, the confusion has reigned even harder and has been more challenging to escape.

That's a shame because few products of the 21st century have more potential and promise than cryptocurrency. Indeed, the people who have paid close attention to the cryptocurrency industry have seen significant growth. It has been growth that needs to be consistent, of course. No one is going to argue that. But it has been growth that has led to terrific financial success and stability for many people. It is also the sort of potential that has invited people new to investing and those who have, until now, never put their money into any market.

Additionally, cryptocurrency has been a great disruptor. More than anything, cryptocurrency has sent a message to many who have long been a part of the investing world. Cryptocurrency has sent a shot across the bow, shaken things up, and shown the young and old world that the status quo doesn't have to be the only way things are. Things can change, and items can be altered, even after generations.

Cryptocurrency has been more than a way for people to make millions of dollars. It has been a way to show the world the potential of technology and new ways of thinking. Make no mistake: cryptocurrency has been more than an asset trading on a radically free market. It has been a message, a silent protest that has still spoken loudly. Anyone who doesn't recognize that ignores cryptocurrency's general concept and ideals.

You would think something as promising and groundbreaking as cryptocurrency would have nothing but fans worldwide. Yet that is not the case. People need help understanding it. Even the most studied and well-versed traders have basic questions. Yes, even those who have studied Wall Street for decades and have made vast fortunes investing, buying, selling, and trading can't even really express what cryptocurrency is.

There are so many legions and legions of people, both professional and not, who need to learn how crypto works, why it works, and what it is about. Confusion reigns, and so does mindless speculation, rumor, and suspicion. Many see cryptocurrency as a fluke, something that isn't real, or some major scam that will steal your money like a pyramid scheme. Indeed, even though the opinions are based on factually incorrect assumptions and a lack of knowledge and research, nearly every belief about cryptocurrency is firm and set in its way.

Despite what people say, cryptocurrency isn't a shady scam created by criminals looking to use the internet to line their pocketbooks or do something horrible. That couldn't be further from the truth. The truth is much more exciting for anyone willing to put money into the market. The truth is that cryptocurrency is one of the best ways to invest, a thoughtful approach to entering a market that is still young and fresh and needs to be adequately valued by many. While scores of people need help understanding cryptocurrency accurately, that is okay for those looking to make money. That is a benefit to you if you are looking to become an active and successful cryptocurrency trader. The more knowledge you have about cryptocurrency, the more power you have. Once you truly understand how it works, why it works, and how it may work in the future, the better your chances to make much money.

You would have been laughed away by experts a decade ago if you asked them whether to invest in a virtual currency. Now, things have turned around. The digitally-coded currency, cryptocurrency, is undisputed and known as the next frontier in the global financial order. Cryptocurrencies will continue to thrive and exist for a very long time because there are over 5000 types in circulation.

Cryptocurrencies are regarded as the most profitable assets within the realm of investments. Cryptocurrency has gradually taken over as the top choice for investors to store their capital, even though it began as a decentralized alternative to the conventional financial system driven by fiat money. Cryptocurrencies such as Bitcoin and Ethereum have established a good reputation. For a currency to be robust, its supply, functionality, security protocol, and acceptability must be in place. One can assess whether cryptocurrency is a good investment by looking into these aspects.

Yes, cryptocurrency has much potential. Some argue that it has more potential than most traditional forms of currency. That is because of what it stands for, its functionality and how it can perform, and the system built to power and protect it.

Yes, the engine behind cryptocurrency is one of the biggest reasons people believe in and invest in cryptocurrency. That engine creates and maintains checks and balances like a well-oiled machine. And that engine, like cryptocurrency itself, is powered by and for the people. The people who use and believe in cryptocurrency are the same people who keep an eye on it and ensure everything is performing smoothly and just like it should.

A significant part of the engine behind cryptocurrency is something called blockchain. In some ways, blockchain is more complicated than cryptocurrency itself. Indeed, it's impossible to deny that blockchain is a massive system that runs like a living and breathing organism that never sleeps and never rests. There are many moving parts - millions of them. However, like cryptocurrency, blockchain's basic premise and concepts aren't that hard to understand. And once you do grasp them and truly see how and why they work, it will open up avenues of investment, saving, and trading that can make you a small fortune.

But blockchain is about more than that, which is precisely why it has so much potential. From healthcare companies to automation to elections to transportation, shipping, and more, blockchain is finding ways to touch upon industries all over the globe. Blockchain is proving what it can do - and how it can alter entire businesses with ease and efficiency. For that reason and many others, blockchain has more potential than can be summarized. It does have the power to change the world ultimately.

Chapter 2: The History of Cryptocurrency

How Did It Start?

Cryptocurrency - and the blockchain system that powers it - has come a long way since it was conceived many years ago. Like all of the greatest inventions of the 21st century and before, these two things started as thoughts, ideas that seemed unachievable but carried great promise from the very beginning. It was later refined, crafted, and created before being put into action. But where did they come from? Why were they made? And why have they always been thought of as revolutionary and radical thoughts and ideas since the beginning?

Desperate times call for desperate measures. If you were alive during the early-to-mid 2000s, you know just how desperate those times were. Sure enough, the chaotic and troubling age of the late 2000s called for the creation of cryptocurrency after years and years of just speculating about it. The status quo had reached a point that was no longer safe or stable, and people were looking to shake it up in some significant, startling ways. That shake-up would lead to the actual implementation of cryptocurrency. In short, it would change the world.

It is essential to remember where things stood economically during that time. Every action is a reaction. The inception of Bitcoin, altcoins, the trading market, and all of the cryptocurrency was a reaction to a system going wildly off the rails.

The US and global economies boomed in the 1990s. The stock market rose, millions of jobs were created, and the internet changed money-making and spending. Millions were happiest. The economy boomed after the late 1980s and early 1990s recession. For the first time in generations, 2000 was exciting and hopeful.

In 2000, many people's finances improved. Global trade was increasing, banks were freed from numerous financial rules that limited their capacity to lend, and the Internet was becoming solid and new. No significant conflicts allowed oil and trade between multiple superpowers.

The internet has grown constantly. Websites grew overnight. Amazon and Google started well. They have redefined reality. Many couldn't imagine life before such sites.

Internet success helped several major companies. Things escalated. Good things end. After a few years, the dot-com bubble crashed, and many promising sites failed. Early internet businesses evaluated every idea. Many continue. Many perished.

Investors stunned. Even in good times, the market was kind to only some companies. Lows follow highs. Goodness fades.

Homeowners and loan applicants prospered as the internet faltered—years of bank loan difficulties. You required good credit. Due to solid government constraints, US banks must make intelligent decisions with limited lending. Banks battled with 1980s excess. These restrictions prohibited millions of Americans from getting their dream homes. With capital, a bank would accept them.

The early 2000s were different. Washington, DC, made life easier for lenders and bank loan applicants across multiple administrations.

Conservative Americans changed regulations. Structures disappeared ten years ago. The new mindset encouraged rule-breaking and unrestrained enterprise. After years of adjusting, bank lending standards eased in the late 90s and early 00s. Many banks had complete control over lending and amounts. In a significant legislative change, anyone might find a home. Banks lent to many previously unaffordable people. Banks now discounted and repaid hostile credit clients. Nationwide, under-$30,000 buyers bought two-bedroom dwellings.

The cause? Because old rules were removed. Banks have more freedom to boost the economy. Banks signed billions in loans and leases. Americans bought homes and spent to profit. They were still expanding.

Banks profited from mortgages and borrowers in new ways while making more money. Debt benefited them. They sold mortgage debts to other banks when clients defaulted. Banks bought debts. One bank would buy client debt, knowing the consumer or third party would pay it. Debt-buying banks gain anyway. Lending and buying receivables made banks money.

It was an intelligent system that made banks and loan companies unlimited money from others' sorrow. New homeowners' hardship benefited banks. The system collapsed. The corrupted and connected system did it in.

Millions received fraudulent loans and mortgages. Why not? Banks won. They might collect mortgage payments or sell faulty lending and debt to other banks for profit. More chickens returned than expected. New homeowners who couldn't afford their mortgages kept defaulting. Many owed. Late millions due trillions.

The banks lost money since they quickly sold these debts to various financial institutions. Many couldn't pay, and mortgage-based funding needed to be more adequate. Debt sales fell short. Worse, banks and financial institutions buying those debts also suffered. They bought lender debt expecting payment. Bad lenders and borrowers should have paid. Banks lost money.

A financial web exchanged consumer debts. Banks worldwide collaborated, so the idea of one failing was unthinkable. Why so unlikely? Because this had been done for millennia, and if one component of this web disappeared, others would too. Dominoes would crash the financial world—network outage. Greed and money-making have established a community. The single ship sank the fleet. An apocalyptic collapse seemed unfathomable.

Unchecked, it crumbled. The housing bubble burst catastrophically. Homebuyers stopped. Banks and mortgage companies went bankrupt, lending to everyone. After debts, they had nothing. Bad loans and debt purchases cost billions. They couldn't wait. Big banks and companies needed to collect. This was a series of economic tremors that kept coming. Weekly, monthly. Bad financial news piled up, harming the US and global economies. A thousand cuts killed the American economy. They continued. All fell. Things worsened.

Wall Street's biggest names were ensnared in this enormous disaster after trading debt like a commodity. Wall Street Titans struggled. All connected. Banks, brokerages, mortgage lenders, etc. Everyone died instantly.

Loans stopped, affecting more businesses worldwide. Business stops without money. Banks needed to be more vital to lend or take risks. After banks stopped financing, companies worldwide cut spending, hours, and staff. All froze. Many successful enterprises failed because banks wouldn't lend them money. During an exceptional recession, some big corporations sacked employees at an alarming rate. Money disappeared. No one could borrow, lend, work, or depend on banks.

Media and the economy wreaked havoc daily. In the fall of 2008, a major retailer, bank, or corporation failed daily. Each story was wrecked. Some decades-old brands closed and laid off workers. Unemployment skyrocketed. Many American cities featured tent villages as families were evicted at alarming rates. Influential individuals looked afraid. The same bureaucrats who had relaxed limitations and permitted banks to change laws for their benefit were now fixing everything. Historians witnessed the 1920s Great Depression began. Only this crisis might worsen things beyond that historic low.

Understandable global and American fury. Most people were innocent. Therefore, they felt cheated. Most avoided problematic loans and expensive residences. Most worked and saved. Meanwhile, influential banks and politicians modified the system to generate more money—an unprecedented economic collapse. Most people followed the rules, but the plan was rigged, and its crooked laws put people in dangerous situations. Political conditions should be known to non-attendees. Banks and other financial institutions fell, the economy crumbled, and worry and uncertainty loomed throughout the most excellent American presidential election history. The election cost millions before Wall Street and Main Street crashed. The two leading candidates, Arizona Senator John McCain and Illinois Senator Barack Obama were trying to adapt to this new reality and prove they could restore the economy and instability. George W. Bush cautioned the November 2008 winner of a unique problem. Long-term crisis. It survived the new presidency.

His composure and dedication helped Senator Obama win a landslide victory in November 2008. This historic candidate faced decades-long storms. The president later predicted a deeper economic downturn and shortages not seen since the 1930s. Obama's optimism didn't help.

In 2008, more unmatched institutions failed. CEOs and Washington power brokers' incompetence and shadiness broke these massive corporations. Many other businesses would follow if they failed, destroying the economy for decades. The spider web was unraveling, the dominoes were falling, and the US government had a choice: let them all collapse and wreck the global economy, reducing the US into a third-world country overnight, or keep these businesses propped up with American tax dollars. The government chose the latter in one of the most controversial American moments.

Many were unhappy that the government bailed out big banks, lenders, and Wall Street titans. Most Americans realized that the world would have entered a dark financial age if nothing were done, yet many were dissatisfied with Congress and the president's choice. Why support Wall Street when Main Street suffers more? Why were bankers and lenders hired while others waited in unemployment lines? Betrayed, approval ratings dropped. These enormous firms breached the regulations and got away with gluttonous, greedy deeds, yet they were paid abundantly while struggling workers lost their jobs for something they didn't do.

No one was convicted. The economy revived after millions of jobs and businesses closed. Wall Street and big banks were exempt. Congress called witnesses, and some lost high-paying careers, but nothing changed. They were breaking the rules. Hedge fund managers and CEOs flaunted their wealth and lawlessness while making millions. No judges or juries saw them. They got off. The corruption that produced the most significant recession since the 1930s was still present.

The Great Recession raised questions. Many discussed our system. System creators profited. Why? Why did citizens need authorities? Profiting how? Millionaires benefitting from homebuyers' pain? Why wasn't anyone safeguarding the tiny family promised a mortgage by a bank that knew they shouldn't?

How did the system become so corrupt? The chaos caused a financial catastrophe. Worst hit? US citizen. Criminals exploited them. Criminals ran Wall Street and banks. As indicated, the crooks didn't care and kept power as the average American struggled.

Millions raged. Washington's politics and system were detested. Corruption increased. Many witnessed unpunished crimes but felt helpless. How do you change a vast, embedded system? They couldn't leave. They rejected a financial plan that rewarded the undeserving.

They'd escape how? Alternatives to American and global banks were impossible. The establishment seemed to have the upper hand against innovation. Restarting looked hard. It was like acquiring a DMV license to use a different currency. Nobody knew how.

Suddenly, ideas that had existed in the deepest reaches of the internet for ages took on new life and had new interest shined on them. There had been talking of an alternative to traditional currency and the system that used it, this talk had existed for years and years, but it never amounted to more than gossip and speculation, the sort of thing message boards online specialized in. In certain internet circles, people had spoken and written about an all-digital form of money that would only be used online. It wouldn't be printed; it couldn't be held. It would break free from the powerful, restrictive, corrupt system that caused many problems. It would be a currency that was for the people, by the people. If someone could figure out how to create and implement a system like this, they could introduce millions to a whole new way to make, save, spend, and buy.

But how could that be done? How could anyone create a system of an all-digital currency? How could anyone monitor it and ensure it wasn't taken advantage of and misused? No one was under the impression that only the rich and powerful on Wall Street were the ones who could grow corrupt. Great power and wealth create a desire for more, often leading to people breaking the rules, breaking the law, and doing everything to advance their means.

It was plain that an all-digital currency would be worthwhile if it could be practical. Yet, despite all the talk of this online currency, no one knew how to create and make it work. All the presented options relied upon old institutions many were trying to move away from, such as banks and the government. Those who proposed a digital currency didn't want anything to do with those powers, so they created this idea in the first place.

Then, in 2008, everything changed when one man, or a group of people, proposed what would become Bitcoin. With just some simple keystrokes and a few new ideas, fantasy became a reality that has changed our world for the better.

The Birth of Bitcoin

The concept of a digital currency has been talked about before by many different people all over the internet. However, the central ideas that would eventually transform into Bitcoin and cryptocurrency were introduced on October 31, 2008, days before the presidential election and amid the Great Recession. These thoughts and solid plans were submitted by a person or group named Satoshi Nakamoto. You may be asking yourself, who is Satoshi Nakamoto? The simple answer is that no one knows. Since Nakamoto would never reveal their or their identity, the name remains shrouded in true mystery. One person or group could use a single word to produce their content. Many assume that Satoshi Nakamoto was a pseudonym used by individuals who shared the single, strong idea to overhaul the banking system with the working concept of cryptocurrency. It doesn't matter who Nakamoto was because the thoughts they created speak louder than an identity; they are far more significant than just one person or one name.

Nakamoto started a movement with just the click of his mouse. He created a post on a cryptography mailing list called "Bitcoin P2P e-cash paper." The title was bland, but the information therein was revolutionary. A link took readers to a paper called "Bitcoin: A Peer-to-Peer Electronic Cash System." That substantial paper laid out the plans and the functionality of what would become Bitcoin. Unlike many other online debates, Nakamoto's paper was written with original, thought-out concepts mixed with hard facts. It poses questions - and answers - that hadn't been heard or thought of before. It wasn't just some out-of-this-world idea; it showed how cryptocurrency could be implemented, monitored, and run safely and effectively. To those who had spoken of this vague idea of cryptocurrency for a long time, Nakamoto's paper was akin to the creation of the wheel or the discovery of fire.

Nakamoto's plan was based on a series of "coins" or "tokens." These coins could be sent across the network from user to user without employing a single administrator to keep tabs on them. No banks, governments, or financial powerhouses run or use the system to their advantage.

The paper also brought another brand new concept to the table, one that changed everything: blockchain. To make this radical, all-digital system work, the system would need some all-digital ledger to keep things in line. Without banks doing the paperwork, there stood a chance that people could game the system or otherwise not keep track of who was sending whom money and how much that money was worth. It had been done before with traditional currency; why wouldn't it happen with Bitcoin if it wasn't kept in check?

That led to the inclusion of blockchain. Like a hard-bound paper book you would find in a bank, blockchain is an online ledger used across an entire network of computers participating in the system. It is not owned or run by one group or person. Instead, blockchain runs itself and constantly updates all transactions' history. It is impossible to be tampered with and is a safe, secure, and anonymous way for the cryptocurrency world to keep moving. Everyone who participates owns the blockchain, which is spread worldwide, making it safer than one centralized history of all the Bitcoin transactions.

Blockchain was almost as revolutionary as Bitcoin and cryptocurrency itself. It was a new technology, a way to tie transactions together and turn them into a series of blocks. The way that every transaction is secured together (hence the word "chain") means that if you change one trade, you change them all. That means you cannot modify any block without altering the rest of the chain. This is terrible news for anyone trying to hack or tweak the system for their advantage. Essentially all Bitcoin users expand upon an incredibly long line of code every time they make a transaction. Every piece of the chain, known as hashes, relies on one another; they are all linked in ways that cannot be pulled apart. They work together in a way that makes them more secure and impossible to be tweaked after the fact. It is one long chain and cannot exist without another. Each chain piece is shared; every computer with the blockchain code has *all* of it.

As stated, the blockchain is not stored in one central location, like a vault in a bank. Instead, it is distributed among all the users of the system. Everyone has a copy of this blockchain and spreads and refreshes it whenever a new transaction is added to the network. Instead of one bank vault, think of it as millions of lockers applying worldwide. But unless you can access all of them unnoticed and simultaneously, none will be worth it. The web of computers running the blockchain made it nearly impossible to be hacked or toyed with.

Blockchain is a reliable and safe way of recording any transactions. It does away with the need for external authority, which is one of the reasons why so many people were attracted to the idea. Bitcoin users did not need to report to a third party every time they made a transaction. Instead, they relied upon the ever-evolving blockchain and other Bitcoin users to keep everything robust, healthy, and safe. This concept was new and revolutionary, taking the idea of cryptocurrency and making it realistic and even possible. With these secure checkpoints, the cryptocurrency could be established and flourish.

Blockchain was the missing puzzle piece that tied everything together and took Bitcoin into a realm previously possible cryptocurrencies never achieved. A plan and a real cryptocurrency with a blueprint for success could now be followed. Blockchain did away with the worries that cryptocurrency would be unregulated and completely unsafe; it was no longer considered a Wild West landscape for the modern age. Instead, it was now safer than traditional money. If implemented, this plan would rely upon the people using Bitcoin. They would be the enforcers, the vanguards, the safety that kept the entire system honest and robust. This was a brilliant idea, turning the champions and most significant fans of cryptocurrency into the guardians and protectors of it. Who better than them to run things and ensure everything went smoothly and safely? These people had the most skin in the game; it only made sense that they were the most involved.

Nakamoto's concepts of Bitcoin, especially the inclusion of blockchain, made many people all over the globe excited. Finally, written in precise detail and understandable language, was the definitive idea that so many people had rallied behind for years: the premise of a digitized currency that was for the people and by the people and did not rely on banks. The safety installed by blockchain made the belief even more tantalizing for so many. Digital currency proponents would finally have a strong, tested concept that could stand independently. They took to the critics and showed them that not only was cryptocurrency safe, but it was also possible.

And then, Bitcoin was born, and cryptocurrency was introduced to the world. On January 3, 2009, the Bitcoin network officially started when Nakamoto created, or "mined," the first block of Bitcoin, block 0. Australian programmer Hal Finley was the first person to receive any bitcoins. He downloaded the Bitcoin software on the first day and received ten bitcoins from Nakamoto for his troubles. That transaction, which occurred on January 12, 2009, was the first Bitcoin transaction ever. Little did the parties involved know just how historic that moment was.

As stated, the blockchain is not stored in one central location, like a vault in a bank. Instead, it is distributed among all the users of the system. Everyone has a copy of this blockchain and spreads and refreshes it whenever a new transaction is added to the network. Instead of one bank vault, think of it as millions of lockers applying worldwide. But unless you can access all of them unnoticed and simultaneously, none will be worth it. The web of computers running the blockchain made it nearly impossible to be hacked or toyed with.

Blockchain is a reliable and safe way of recording any transactions. It does away with the need for external authority, which is one of the reasons why so many people were attracted to the idea. Bitcoin users did not need to report to a third party every time they made a transaction. Instead, they relied upon the ever-evolving blockchain and other Bitcoin users to keep everything robust, healthy, and safe. This concept was new and revolutionary, taking the idea of cryptocurrency and making it realistic and even possible. With these secure checkpoints in place, cryptocurrency could be established and flourish.

Blockchain was the missing puzzle piece that tied everything together and took Bitcoin into a realm previously possible cryptocurrencies never achieved. A plan and a real cryptocurrency with a blueprint for success could now be followed. Blockchain did away with the worries that cryptocurrency would be unregulated and completely unsafe; it was no longer considered a Wild West landscape for the modern age. Instead, it was now safer than traditional money. If implemented, this plan would rely upon the people using Bitcoin. They would be the enforcers, the vanguards, the safety that kept the entire system honest and robust. This was a brilliant idea, turning the champions and most significant fans of cryptocurrency into the guardians and protectors of it. Who better than them to run things and ensure everything went smoothly and safely? These people had the most skin in the game; it only made sense that they were the most involved.

Nakamoto's concepts of Bitcoin, especially the inclusion of blockchain, made many people all over the globe excited. Finally, written in precise detail and understandable language, was the definitive idea that so many people had rallied behind for years: the premise of a digitized currency that was for the people and by the people and did not rely on banks. The safety installed by blockchain made the belief even more tantalizing for so many. Digital currency proponents would finally have a strong, tested concept that could stand independently. They took to the critics and showed them that not only was cryptocurrency safe, but it was also possible.

And then, Bitcoin was born, and with it, cryptocurrency was introduced to the world. On January 3, 2009, the Bitcoin network officially started when Nakamoto created, or "mined," the first block of Bitcoin, block 0. Australian programmer Hal Finley was the first person to receive any bitcoins. He downloaded the Bitcoin software on the first day and received ten bitcoins from Nakamoto for his troubles. That transaction, which occurred on January 12, 2009, was the first Bitcoin transaction ever. Little did the parties involved know just how historic that moment was.

How much was Bitcoin worth on its opening day? Very little, almost next to nothing. Yet, the amount was agreed on in a very democratic and fair way. The people using the Bitcoin forums decided and negotiated the value of these first Bitcoin transactions. They would debate, argue, agree, and come together with an appropriate amount everyone saw eye-to-eye on. Again, that proved that Bitcoin was and will always be a form of currency that kept the people using it front-and-center and always in control. Even from its start, Bitcoin strongly emphasized being a democratic and decentralized form of payment that would always put the people first.

Bitcoin was born, but its future was uncertain from the very start. In time, it would be repeatedly proven that its future would often remain uncertain. Where would it go next? The same power would dictate the future the past had been: the people who cared most about Bitcoin on both sides of the argument. The fight for and against Bitcoin had just begun.

Bitcoin was just a promising but unreadable idea when Satoshi Nakamoto published his paper on creating, managing, and maintaining Bitcoin. From there, things moved quickly, and the first coin was made on January 3, 2009.

After the creation of the first Bitcoin, the system began to come to life and live on its own, a system that would rise or fall based solely on the involvement of those championing it and participating in it.

For the first few years of Bitcoin, the value of Bitcoin has remained low. It was incredibly, incredibly low. In the beginning, a single Bitcoin was valued at only $0.003. The distance it has come since then is truly astronomical.

Though the cost of Bitcoin was meager in its early days, people didn't know how to use it. They didn't know how to obtain it. They didn't know how to determine the value of it. Although the person or group called Satoshi Nakamoto had laid out the blueprint for Bitcoin, he didn't stick around long to see how far it would go. In 2011, Nakamoto stepped away from Bitcoin to work on other projects. He has not been heard from since, and because of his anonymous true identity, he has never been found. The creator of Bitcoin disappeared right as his baby was becoming a toddler.

The early days of Bitcoin were wild and most casual. People who could get Bitcoins would trade them or use them to buy commodities from others in the community. In May 2010, a Florida programmer named Laszlo Hanyec offered 10,000 Bitcoins in exchange for some Papa John's pizza. A British Bitcoin fan took him up on the offer and sent two pizzas to Hanyec's home. That date, May 22, 2010, is now called Bitcoin Pizza Day. To many, it is believed to be the first time Bitcoin was ever used to make an actual purchase. The Bitcoins didn't buy the pizzas; the British fan's credit card did. But it was the first time that Bitcoins were used to receive goods or services. In 2010, 10,000 Bitcoins were worth the value of two large pizzas. Times have changed dramatically since then.

Around the same time as Bitcoin Pizza Day, users online determined that they needed to establish some online exchange system to trade and easily buy Bitcoin honestly. They took note of techniques such as the stock market and trading sites that quickly allowed clients to buy, sell, and trade their stocks. If sites like these could be created for Bitcoin, proponents believed that you would see a significant number of people looking to buy and sell and grow the popularity of Bitcoin.

Bitcoinmarket.com was launched on January 15, 2010, by a user on a Bitcoin message board. The site was rudimentary at first, but it was also an incredible feat and a step forward for the future of Bitcoin. On the site, people could buy Bitcoin at a user-determined price. This would be the way that people decided upon the value of Bitcoin. It would use the most basic principles of capitalism and supply and demand. If people wanted to spend more on Bitcoins, they could. If people thought it didn't have as much value, their financial offer would express that.

This was a significant moment for Bitcoin. It was when things started moving forward, and the new currency's actual, easy-to-understand value was founded. By simply supply and demand and speculative opinion from users, Bitcoin was gaining a true sense of worth. As mentioned, it wasn't a lot. In the early days, a single Bitcoin cost less than a penny. But as time passed, the same fundamental ideas established at that early trading site would carry forward into others. There will be multiple other ways to buy, trade, and speculate on Bitcoin in just a few years. The value would only go up and up too. But it all started in those early days of 2010 when an anonymous user took it upon themself to create a site to dictate the Bitcoin market.

This was another example of Bitcoin being for and by the people. In the beginning, no one knew how much a Bitcoin was worth. No one knew if the man who received his pizzas and spent 10,000 Bitcoins to get them was being ripped off or receiving a great deal. No one knew if $0.003 was too high or too low for a Bitcoin. It was all up in the air, nothing was determined, and nothing was certain.

But the system worked itself out, not with the help of any government bank too. The people who believed in Bitcoin stepped forward and showed their faith in the ideas proposed just months before by creating a system that would keep the entire concept of Bitcoin alive. None of this would have happened if it weren't for the people. If it weren't for the people, the future of Bitcoin would have collapsed in such uncertainty. As it stands now, the people were the ones that believed in Bitcoin and pushed it forward.

In the weeks, months, and years after its creation, the value of Bitcoin continued to rise. As Bitcoin was now trading on an online exchange and consumers were selecting a price for the currency, it was finding a footing with others, not only those who had championed it before it existed.

If you look at the price history of Bitcoin, you can see the progress it has made. The excitement of its buyers has always influenced Bitcoin's value, but there was a time when that enthusiasm needed to translate into a high value. When Bitcoin was first introduced, it was worth less than a penny. Eventually, it was worth more than that, but only by a little.

Bitcoin was just $1 in April 2011, a few years ago. That was a significant moment for the cryptocurrency, proving it was competitive with the dollar. Bitcoins were meant to grow much more valuable than just a single dollar in the future. Some naysayers never imagined it would have progressed that far. It was a watershed moment when it equaled a dollar, but it was only the beginning.

It wasn't until 2011 that Bitcoin showed just how volatile it could be. Bitcoin's wild fluctuations in value are a recurring theme. When you look at a chart of the price of Bitcoin over time, you will see highs as high as the sky and lows as steep as the earth. There have been a lot of ups and downs, ups and downs, and ups and downs since creation. In general, its volatility is much greater than that of most other currencies. This was also true in 2011 when Bitcoin experienced enormous gains...and losses.

It was a big deal when Bitcoin reached $1 in April 2011. Only after Bitcoin's price increased this became a bigger deal. When Bitcoin hit $32 in June of that year, the value was almost three times what it was in January. The gain in a few months was nearly 3,200%. Bitcoin enthusiasts were ecstatic, seeing this as a sign that cryptocurrency was catching on faster than expected and their ground-floor investments would pay off big. The timing was right for many of them, they felt. It was only upwards, upwards.

However, those familiar with trading markets, and those who recognize that there are peaks and valleys in trading any commodity, assumed that this ascent would only last for a while. Bitcon's price would likely plummet shockingly fast. Sure enough, Bitcoin's value dropped to $2 in November 2011, just a few months after reaching its high of $32. At the beginning of that year, Bitcoin was worth $1. By the summer, it was worth $32; at the end of the year, it was worth just $2. For investors, this was quite the wild ride and the moment that stood out for those who thought Bitcoin's prices would only rise. The exchange rate reminded us that currency values change quickly, only sometimes in your favor. This lesson was an important wake-up call to the many Bitcoin fans investing for the first time: don't assume anything is a sure thing, and only sometimes expect success. Even with something you genuinely believe in, investing is not guaranteed.

This was when I opened my account at Coinbase. If I had funded it in 2012, I would not have had to write books about it to make money.

As the year 2012 wore on, Bitcoin's value steadily rose. It reached nearly $5 in May and then $13.20 by the summer of that year. The Bitcoin community agreed that the cryptocurrency was headed in the right direction. Would the drops become more rapid in the future?

Many online exchanges, message boards, and stories have been written about cryptocurrency, especially Bitcoin, as it grew in popularity. Bitcoin was becoming widespread worldwide, and its early adoption was considered helpful in getting in on it as soon as possible. In Bitcoin's early years, there were substantial and often reliable gains. Bitcoin was getting more and more popular.

Chapter 3: Blockchain 101 - What Is It?

Blockchain in Simple Terms

If you are trying to wrap your head around cryptocurrency and blockchain, it is essential that you break it down to its basic components, its base ideas, and concepts. This knowledge will be very valued if you attempt to carve a path for yourself in the investing world or want to explain blockchain and cryptocurrency to others who don't understand it.

Knowing how to summarize concepts in simple, basic terms is essential when educating others and yourself. Even the most complex ideas and institutions can be broken down into simple terms and conveyed in ways everyone can understand. The same is true for blockchain and its system: cryptocurrency.

The truth is that many people don't venture into the world of cryptocurrency because they are afraid of it. Why are they scared of it? Simply because they don't know how to wrap their heads around it. They don't understand it. They don't see how it works, why it works, or why it would be worth their time and effort.

It may seem not very easy, and it can be, but its core concept is quite simple. An example of a blockchain is a database. To understand blockchain, one must first understand what a database is.

An electronic database is a collection of information stored on a computer system. Databases typically contain information in table form so that searching for specific information is more accessible. Is it different from using a spreadsheet instead of a database to store data?

A spreadsheet is designed to store and make access to the limited information available to one person or a small group. By contrast, a database is designed to hold a significant amount of data multiple users can access, filter, and manipulate simultaneously.

The data is stored on powerful computers in large databases. For an extensive database to be accessible simultaneously, these servers may use hundreds of computers to provide the computational power and storage capacity. Usually, a spreadsheet or database is owned by a business and managed by a specific individual with access to all the data.

What is the difference between a blockchain and a database?

Well, there are, in fact, many differences. One key difference between a typical database and a blockchain is how the data is structured. A blockchain collects information together in groups, also known as blocks, that hold sets of information. Blocks have specific storage capacities and, when filled, are chained onto the previously served block, forming a data chain known as the "blockchain." All new information that follows that freshly added block is compiled into a newly formed block that will be added to the chain once filled.

Unlike a database that structures data into tables, a blockchain, as its name implies, structures its data into chunks (blocks) linked together. In other words, not all databases are blockchains, but all blockchains are databases. When implemented in a decentralized manner, this system creates an irreversible timeline of data. Once a block is filled, it is set in stone and becomes part of this timeline. A partnership is given an exact timestamp when added to the chain.

The implementation of blockchain by Bitcoin provides a helpful context to comprehend blockchain. Bitcoin's blockchain is stored on a collection of computers, just like a database. The blockchain in Bitcoin acts as a database for saving every Bitcoin transaction ever made. This is not the case with most databases, and in Bitcoin's case, each compute node is controlled by an individual or a small group of individuals.

Assume a company owns a server with 10,000 computers and a database with all its clients' account information. They have a warehouse with all of these computers under one roof and complete control over each of them and the data stored on them. Like Bitcoin, Bitcoin includes thousands of computers, each of which holds a blockchain in a different geographic location and is operated by an individual or group of individuals. Bitcoin's network is composed of computers called nodes.

Using Bitcoin's blockchain as a decentralized database is part of this model. It is possible for private, centralized blockchains, which are made up of computers owned and controlled by one entity, to exist.

Each node records the data stored on a blockchain since it began. The data for Bitcoin consists of the entire history of all Bitcoin transactions. Thousands of other nodes can be a reference if one node has an error in its data.o, correct it. The network is thus protected from being altered by any one node within it. This means that every transaction in a block of the Bitcoin blockchain cannot be reversed.

One user could tamper with Bitcoin's history of transactions, and all the other nodes would quickly identify the node with incorrect data. We can establish a transparent and precise order of events using this system. Blockchains can hold a myriad of information, including transactions for Bitcoin, state identifications, and company inventories.

A majority of the decentralized network's computing power would be required to change how the system operates or the information it contains. Whenever changes do occur, it is in the majority's best interests.

Due to the decentralized nature of Bitcoin's blockchain, all transactions can be viewed transparently by using an individual node or blockchain explorers that allow anyone to see the live transactions. Each node gets its copy as new blocks are confirmed and added to the chain. Therefore, bitcoin could be tracked wherever it goes.

For example, exchanges have been hacked, resulting in Bitcoin holders losing everything they had. Despite the hacker's anonymity, the Bitcoins they extracted are easily traceable. It would be known where some of the Bitcoins stolen in some of these hacks went if they were moved or spent.

In several ways, blockchain technology addresses issues of security and trust. First of all, new blocks are always stored linearly and chronologically. Therefore, they are always tacked onto the end of the blockchain. As of November 2020, the block's height had reached 656,197. Each block on Bitcoin's blockchain has a position on the chain called a "height."

Unless the majority reaches a consensus to change the contents of an added block, it is nearly impossible to go back in time and alter a previously added block. This is because each block has its hash, the previous block, and a time stamp. Digital information is converted to a string of numbers and letters using a mathematical function. Whenever the data is altered, the hash code also changes.

That's why security depends on it. Let us imagine that a hacker wants to steal Bitcoin from everyone by modifying the blockchain. They would have to change their copy, or everyone else's copy would be out of alignment. The rest of the world would see this one copy stand out when they cross-reference their documents, making that hacker's version look rubbish.

The hacker would need to simultaneously control and alter 51% of the blockchain copies so that their copy becomes the majority and, thus, the agreed-upon chain. In addition to the time and resources needed to orchestrate an attack, they would have to rewrite the code for all the blocks since the timestamps and hashes would differ.

Due to the size of Bitcoin's network and its fast-growing, the cost to pull off such a feat would probably be insurmountable. Not only would this be extremely expensive, but it would also likely be fruitless. Doing such a thing would not go unnoticed, as network members would see such drastic alterations to the blockchain. The network members would then fork off to a new chain version unaffected.

This would cause the attacked version of Bitcoin to plummet in value, making the attack ultimately pointless as the lousy actor has control of a worthless asset. The same would occur if the awful actor attacked the new Bitcoin fork. It is built this way so that participating in the network is far more economically incentivized than attacking it.

The Origins of Blockchain

Blockchain aims to allow digital information to be recorded and distributed, but not edited. Blockchain technology was first outlined in 1991 by Stuart Haber and W. Scott Stornetta, two researchers who wanted to implement a system where document timestamps could not be tampered with. But After almost 20 years, Bitcoin's launch in January 2009 was the first time blockchain was used for real-life purposes.

A blockchain is the foundation of the Bitcoin protocol. Satoshi Nakamoto, the pseudonymous creator of Bitcoin, called the digital currency "a new electronic cash system that is fully peer-to-peer and without any trusted third parties."

Bitcoin uses blockchain to record payments transparently, but theoretically, it can record any number of quantities immutably. This may be a transaction, a vote in an election, a product inventory, a state identification, a deed for a home, and more.

Several blockchain-based projects are exploring using blockchain for more than just recording transactions. A good example is the use of blockchains for democratized elections. As a result of blockchain's immutability, fraudulent voting would become much less likely.

For instance, each country's citizen could be issued a cryptocurrency or token as a voting system. Upon receiving a wallet address, each candidate would be given their own, and their tokens or cryptocurrency would then be sent to that address. Due to blockchain's transparent and traceable nature, voting would no longer require human intervention, and no physical ballots could be tampered with.

Advantages and Disadvantages of Blockchain

Blockchain is a revolutionary creation that powers cryptocurrencies and can transform other industries for the better.

Even with its upsides and advantages, blockchain has some disadvantages. Knowing both is necessary to grasp blockchain's potential and abilities fully.

It is important to note that many people rail against blockchain and all cryptocurrency and think it is dangerous and should be illegal. We will discuss that are more length soon. But it is also vital to understand that many issues people have with blockchain and cryptocurrency, valid or not, are overblown. And more importantly, many things that bother people about these two technological marvels can be found in just about any other form of currency on Earth. As you see all the annoying things about blockchain, you will see that that can be applied to the Dollar, the Yen, and so much more.

The truth is that there are advantages and disadvantages to all forms of currency and the systems that run them. That is not unique solely to blockchain and cryptocurrency. That can be admitted and addressed without completely discounting the importance of both. So while blockchain does indeed have many good *and* bad things, they are not the big, scary deal breakers that some people in power make them out to be.

The Advantages of Blockchain

Accuracy of the Chain

A network of thousands of computers approves transactions on the blockchain network. Almost all human input is removed during verification, resulting in less human error and more accurate data. A computational mistake made by one computer on the network would only affect some of the blockchains. It would take at least 51 percent of the computers on the web to make that mistake, which would be nearly impossible on a rapidly expanding network like Bitcoin's.

Cost Reductions

Customers typically pay a bank for a transactional confirmation, a notary for a document signature, or a minister for a marriage ceremony. By eliminating third-party verification, blockchain eliminates associated costs. A small fee is charged to business owners when they accept credit card payments, for example, since banks and payment processing companies handle these transactions. In contrast, Bitcoin is decentralized and offers low transaction fees.

Decentralization

There is no central location for storing blockchain information. An electronic network of computers copies and distributes the blockchain. Any change to the blockchain is reflected on each computer on the web. Blockchain is more difficult to tamper with because the information is spread across several networks rather than centralized. A hacker could only access one copy of the blockchain rather than the entire network if they received a copy.

Efficient Transactions

It can take a few days for transactions completed through a central authority to settle. If you attempt to deposit a check on Friday, it could take until Monday morning to see the funds in your account. Blockchain works 24 hours a day, seven days a week, 365 days a year, unlike financial institutions, which operate five days a week during business hours. The transaction can be completed in as little as ten minutes and considered secure after only a few hours. A benefit of this is that it can be used in cross-border trades, which typically take longer due to time zone differences, and all parties must confirm payment processing.

Private Transactions

The transaction history of some blockchain networks is accessible to anyone with an internet connection because they function as public databases. Users can access transaction information but cannot see an individual's identity. There is a common misconception that blockchain networks like Bitcoin are anonymous. They are not, but at the same time, they still mostly are.

When users make public transactions, their unique code, called a public key, is recorded on the blockchain rather than their personal information. If a person has made a Bitcoin purchase on an exchange requiring identification, their identity is still linked to their blockchain address. Still, a transaction, even when tied to a person's name, does not reveal personal information.

Secure Transactions

The blockchain network must verify the authenticity of a transaction once it has been recorded. On the blockchain, thousands of computers confirm the correct purchase details. Computers validate transactions and add them to the blockchain. In a blockchain, each block has its unique hash and the previous block's hash. Editing information on a block will affect the hashcode of that block but not the hashcode of a block after that. This discrepancy can only change Information on the blockchain with prior notice.

Transparency

Most blockchains are entirely open-source software. This means that anyone and everyone can view its code. This gives auditors the ability to review cryptocurrencies like Bitcoin for security. This also means there is no absolute authority on who controls Bitcoin's code or how it is edited. Because of this, anyone can suggest changes or upgrades to the system. If most network users agree that the new version of the code with the promotion is sound and worthwhile, then Bitcoin can be updated.

Banking the Unbanked

Perhaps the most profound facet of blockchain and Bitcoin is the ability for anyone, regardless of ethnicity, gender, or cultural background, to use it. According to the world bank, nearly 2 billion adults do not have bank accounts or any means of storing their money or wealth.[5] Nearly all of these individuals live in developing countries where the economy is in its infancy and entirely dependent on cash.

These people often earn little money that is paid in physical cash. They then need to store this physical cash in hidden locations in their homes or places of living, subjecting them to robbery or unnecessary violence. Keys to a Bitcoin wallet can be stored on paper, a cheap cell phone, or even memorized if necessary. For most people, these options are likely more easily hidden than a small pile of cash under a mattress.

Blockchains of the future are also looking for solutions to not only be a unit of account for wealth storage but also to store medical records, property rights, and a variety of other legal contracts.

Disadvantages of Blockchain

While there are significant upsides to the blockchain, there are also significant challenges to its adoption. The roadblocks to applying blockchain technology today are more than just technical. The real challenges are political and regulatory, mostly to say nothing of the thousands of hours (read: money) of custom software design and back-end programming required to integrate blockchain into current business networks. Here are some of the challenges standing in the way of widespread blockchain adoption.

The Costs

Although blockchain can save users money on transaction fees, the technology is far from free. For example, Bitcoin's "proof of work" system to validate transactions consumes vast computational power. In the real world, the energy from the millions of computers on the Bitcoin network is close to what Denmark consumes annually. Assuming electricity costs of

$0.03~$0.05 per kilowatt-hour, mining costs, excluding hardware expenses, are about $5,000~$7,000 per coin.

Despite the costs of mining Bitcoin, users continue to drive up their electricity bills to validate blockchain transactions. That's because when miners add a block to the Bitcoin blockchain, they are rewarded with enough Bitcoin to make their time and energy worthwhile. However, miners must be paid or otherwise incentivized to validate transactions regarding blockchains that do not use cryptocurrency.

Some solutions to these issues are beginning to arise. For example, bitcoin mining farms have been set up to use solar power, excess natural gas from fracking sites, or energy from wind farms.

The Speed

Bitcoin is a perfect case study for the possible inefficiencies of blockchain. Bitcoin's "proof of work" system takes about ten minutes to add a new block to the blockchain. At that rate, it's estimated that the blockchain network can only manage about seven transactions per second (TPS). Although other cryptocurrencies, such as Ethereum, perform better than Bitcoin, blockchain still limits them. Legacy brand Visa, for context, can process 24,000 TPS.

Solutions to this issue have been in development for years. There are currently blockchains that boast over 30,000 transactions per second.

Illegal Activity

While confidentiality on the blockchain network protects users from hacks and preserves privacy, it also allows for illegal trading and activity on the blockchain network. The most cited example of blockchain being used for illicit transactions is probably the Silk Road, an online "dark web" drug marketplace operating from February 2011 until October 2013, when the FBI shut it down.

The website allowed users to browse without being tracked using the Tor browser and make illegal purchases in Bitcoin or other cryptocurrencies. Current U.S. regulations require financial service providers to obtain information about their customers when they open an account, verify the identity of each customer, and confirm that customers do not appear on any list of known or suspected terrorist organizations. This system can be seen as both a pro and a con. It gives anyone access to financial accounts and allows criminals to transact more efficiently. Many have argued that the good uses of crypto, like banking the unbanked world, outweigh cryptocurrency's inadequate benefits, primarily when most illegal activity is still accomplished through untraceable cash.

Regulation

Many in the crypto space have expressed concerns about government regulation over cryptocurrencies. While it is getting increasingly tricky and near impossible to end something like Bitcoin as its decentralized network grows, governments could theoretically make it illegal to own cryptocurrencies or participate in their networks.

Over time this concern has grown smaller as large companies like PayPal begin to allow the ownership and use of cryptocurrencies on its platform.

Is Blockchain Safe?

Like everything related to cryptocurrency, many people ask: is it safe? Is blockchain a secure system that delivers on its promise? Or is it too good to be accurate and ready to be hacked and toyed with by criminals looking to make extra money?

The answer is yes, blockchain is safe. It is incredibly safe. What makes it that way? It is a fact that the entire system is entirely decentralized. That means it is located in more than one part of the world. As stated, the computers that run the blockchain system are in homes and businesses across the globe. That is a massive benefit because hackers attempting to access computers must travel worldwide to find them virtually.

This is additionally beneficial because you need to access all of the computers running the blockchain database simultaneously if you hope to break into the system and alter things. Why? Because every computer using blockchain is seeing all the same data in real-time as it evolves and develops and grows. If someone were attempting to break into the system and change it in their favor, they would need to enter somehow every computer running the system and change the growing database so that no other computer would have even a slight variation. If that isn't just about impossible, nothing is.

The blockchain system is safer than safe; it is a Fort Knox vault that will not be broken into or tweaked. It would require the sort of technological magic that isn't possible, nor will it ever be.

What makes blockchain safe is that it is run and monitored, and championed by the same people using it to build their wealth. No one is a bigger fan of blockchain than those looking over it. They need blockchain to invest and trade and buy and sell. They need it to work safely and flawlessly at all times. These people are the system's guardians, using their impressive computer rigs to power the system. They are the ones who need blockchain the most, so they are the ones who will make sure it goes smoothly and smoothly.

Blockchain is a reliable and safe way of recording any transactions. It does away with the need for external authority, which is one of the reasons why so many people were attracted to the idea. Bitcoin users did not need to report to a third party every time they made a transaction. Instead, they relied upon the ever-evolving blockchain and other Bitcoin users to keep everything robust, healthy, and safe. With just a few exceptions, this system worked like a charm.

Nakamoto's idea behind Bitcoin and the inclusion of blockchain made many people all over the globe excited. Finally, written in precise detail and realistic terms, was the idea that so many people had rallied behind for years: the idea of a digitized currency that was for the people and by the people and did not rely on banks. The safety installed by blockchain made the premise even more tantalizing for so many.

Is Cryptocurrency Safe?

This is the question you will be asked again and again. It is one that you will definitely learn the answer to and will believe wholeheartedly. Still, its solution is one to convince some people.

It is worth mentioning repeatedly that cryptocurrency is looked at with suspicion, rumor, and often fear. People don't understand it, and, worst of all, many people seem to fear it. They must learn how something as new and different as cryptocurrency could be safe. The fact that it existed online doesn't help its cause, either. Many investors, including older ones who cut their teeth before the web and were a significant market contributing factor, must see how something solely online can be safe. Isn't it just a big scam? Won't it just steal all your money and leave you nothing?

So, back to the question at hand, the one that will be asked to you repeatedly: are cryptocurrencies safe? The answer to that is a resounding and hearty yes. You can confidently say this and utter the truth whenever you speak it. Cryptocurrencies are incredibly safe. They are often far safer than traditional currencies like the ones we all use currently. Is there a threat of hacking that will rob you of your personal information from the sites you trust most? If we are being honest, we have to say that, yes, there is. However, that is true for any form of money: any bank or institution risks having your information stolen away from them. You do not exist in a world without risks. How often have you heard stories of banks and other major financial institutions falling victim to a significant security breach that gives away millions and millions of customers' information? It happens often. We live in a world where it is a standard part of doing business. So there is risk in all things regarding money; every company, agency, or firm that accepts and stores your money is in the crosshairs of hackers.

However, the idea of cryptocurrency being easily hacked is ludicrous and patently false. As described in the previous section, blockchain technology powering cryptocurrency is nearly impenetrable to almost all hacking schemes. Yes, you may lose your information in a heist, but the overall chance of you losing your valued Bitcoin or another form of cryptocurrency is nearly nonexistent.

Cryptocurrency is safe; it has always been safe and will always be safe. It was created with one of the safest and most secure systems in place: the blockchain. With that, cryptocurrency is not something that can easily be tinkered with. Nor can it easily be stolen away in the dead of night. You may never hold cryptocurrency in your hand, and it may exist only online, but it still needs to be one of Earth's most secure and protected forms of currency.

The fear many people have about the safety of cryptocurrency is unfounded, spurred on by speculation, confusion, ignorance, and sometimes greed by those trying to discredit cryptocurrency. Few things on this earth are safer than holding cryptocurrency.

While cryptocurrency is safe and buying cryptocurrency is too, some risk factors are involved based upon whom you purchase and trade your crypto with. You are investing in and securing your cryptocurrency through online exchanges and websites that act as online marketplaces for buying, trading, and storing your cryptocurrency. When you purchase your share of crypto, you are given a "private key, " a complicated and private string of code used to authorize all outgoing transactions on the blockchain network. Think of your key as a unique ID associated with your cryptocurrency account. It's like your cryptocurrency DNA, only you have it, and it has access to your most valuable information.

We cannot say that your cryptocurrency is safe in every situation because there have been rare times when poorly-made and poorly-regulated online exchanges have allowed themselves to open doors to dangerous schemes.

Unfortunately, hackers have intruded on several online exchanges over the years and have stolen millions of dollars worth of cryptocurrency. This has yet to happen with the more high-end online businesses because they take extra steps to ensure their security is more challenging than their competitors. But it happened at lower-level talks, leading some people to lose valuable investments. It's a rare event that doesn't happen nearly as often as cryptocurrency critics would have you believe. And while some online exchanges cannot get your crypto back for you, others are insured to ensure you are taken care of after a hack. Therefore, while the threat of hacks looms its ugly head occasionally in cryptocurrency, it is okay if you choose a reputable and reliable online exchange. That gives you even more reason to make sure you put your money into a business you can trust, which has repeatedly proven itself to other consumers.

Safety is a significant feature of cryptocurrency. There is the safety of not being tracked by the government and not relying on their outdated system. The safety of the blockchain also ensures that all transactions are accounted for, legitimate, and honest. Then there is the added safety of online exchanges, which have built-in measures to ensure your money doesn't get into the hands of others. Safety is built throughout the cryptocurrency ecosystem; it is downright essential. The cryptocurrency was formed and released into the world when its security and safety were tested, proven, and tested again. The most diehard fans and supporters of cryptocurrency will tell you to be innovative and to make the right choices when it comes to investing and buying. The system will do a lot to keep you safe, but you must do your work too.

Chapter 4: Blockchain & The Market

How Blockchain Changes and Powers the Market

Over the past decade, marketing has undergone many changes; now, it will undergo another revolution, mainly due to blockchain technology. Although most of us associate digital marketing with things like AI and analytics, blockchain might be the most disruptive technology to hit marketers across all industries. You might be surprised at who will benefit from blockchain in digital marketing.

With blockchain technology, two parties can conduct transactions without requiring a third party to verify anything. In finance and cryptocurrencies, blockchain technology has mainly been used, but it could also be used for marketing.

Blockchain allows consumers to regain control of their personal information and thus level the playing field. Here are some ways blockchain is changing digital marketing forever - and for the better.

The most exciting aspect of blockchain is that it returns data value to consumers. In the past, many companies had the advantage of gaining information about their customers. Almost everyone asks for our phone number, email address, and address, as well as our firstborn's name, even when we make a simple purchase in-store or online. This helps the consumer, as it allows them to be targeted by companies. Yet it's also an invasive practice because companies can make money from collecting and sometimes selling the personal data of anyone interacting with their products.

This is simple but revolutionary in terms of digital marketing. The free-for-all data grab is over.

Indeed, if you're in the marketing business, you may not love this concept. In many ways, it's like going back to ground zero—relying on customers to give you the information you want and need to serve them better. Maybe not the best news for digital marketing—but a necessary step forward in terms of consumer protection.

Blockchain technology can do much more than change how people approach and market. Blockchain promises to enable the smooth exchange of information between parties and streamline business processes. Enterprise blockchain can guarantee the accuracy and quality of information, goods, and services and automate contracts.

In a business network, blockchain enhances trust, which allows participants to collaborate without additional guarantees. Companies within the same industry tend to trust one another since they all work towards the same goal of helping the business succeed. It is rare to find that trust between individuals representing different companies, which makes collaboration challenging. A blockchain can build trust and improve processes across multiple organizations.

Eastman Kodak, the legendary camera maker, is an excellent example of how Blockchain can impact businesses. With the introduction of smartphones, the company has struggled to stay competitive. The legacy company was able to reinvent itself with the help of blockchain technology. To create a digital ledger of copyright ownership, the company announced the launch of KODAKOne. Photographers can use the platform to register their old and new work and license it for sale. Through this system, professionals can participate in the new economy of photography by receiving instant, secure payments for their photos.

Accounting can also be radically changed by it. Blockchain technology can be highly beneficial to the field of accounting. Accountancy is filled with challenges - from the overly complex tax code to the need for accuracy and precision. The blockchain can address all of these issues.

The blockchain can reduce auditors' time sampling and validating transactions by providing transparency. Auditors could focus on controls and other vital tasks with more time available.

Blockchain-based systems can also affect pay in multinational corporations and businesses across borders. It simplifies and standardizes payments in different currencies, changing how companies pay their employees. Changing how workers save for retirement can improve employer care.

Workchain, a decentralized protocol for the work economy, presented a tremendous blockchain-based payroll system. Using Workchain, employees can get their paycheck as soon as they complete their work. At the same time, employers can reduce costs and improve efficiency with an automated payroll solution.

A worker is another example of an HR use case; a multi-chain validated data protocol for application creation that simplifies the design and management of applications based on verified data and reputation scores. As a result of Aworker's flexibility, public blockchains can be customized for various applications.

What Is Cryptography?

Cryptography is the study of secure communications techniques that allow only the sender and intended recipient to see the content of a message. The term derives from the Greek word Kryptos, which means hidden. Cryptography involves scrambling ordinary text into what is known as ciphertext, then converting it back to plain text upon delivery. Also included in cryptography is the obfuscation of information in images using microdots or merging. One of the first modern ciphers is credited to Julius Caesar for using one of these methods in complex hieroglyphics.

Most commonly, cryptography is used to encrypt and decrypt plain-text emails and other electronic data. An asymmetric or "secret key" system is the simplest method. A secret key encrypts data, and the encoded message and key are sent to the recipient for decryption. What's the problem? When a message is intercepted, a third party has access to everything they need to decrypt and read the news. Therefore, asymmetric critical systems were invented by cryptologists. Each user has two keys: a public and a private key. Senders encrypt messages and send them along with the recipient's public key. When the message arrives, only the recipient's private key can decode it - which means theft is ineffective without the corresponding private key. Despite malicious third parties–known as adversaries–cryptography offers secure communication. Combining an algorithm and key can transform an input (plaintext) into an encrypted output. When the same key is used with a given algorithm, the plaintext will continually be transformed into the same ciphertext.

Algorithms are considered secure if an attacker cannot determine any properties of the plaintext or key, given the ciphertext. An attacker should not be able to determine anything about a key, given many plaintext/ciphertext combinations that use the key.

There are two different types of cryptography: symmetric and asymmetric. What are they, how do they work, and why do they matter?

With symmetric cryptography, the same key is used for encryption and decryption. A sender and a recipient must already have a shared key known to both. Key distribution is a tricky problem and was the impetus for developing asymmetric cryptography.

With asymmetric crypto, two different keys are used for encryption and decryption. Every user in an asymmetric cryptosystem has a public and private key. The private key is always kept secret, but the public key may be freely distributed. Data encrypted with a public key may only be decrypted with the corresponding private key. So, sending a message to John requires encrypting that message with John's public key. Only John can interpret the news, as only John has his private key. Any data encrypted with a private key can only be solved with the corresponding public key. Similarly, Jane could digitally sign a message with her private key, and anyone with Jane's public key could decrypt the signed message and verify that it was, in fact, Jane who sent it.

Symmetric is generally very fast and ideal for encrypting large amounts of data. Asymmetric is much slower and can only encrypt pieces of data smaller than the critical size (typically 2048 bits or smaller). Thus, asymmetric crypto is generally used to encrypt symmetric encryption keys, which are then used to encrypt much larger data blocks. For digital signatures, asymmetric crypto is usually used to encrypt the hashes of messages rather than entire messages.

A cryptosystem provides for managing cryptographic keys, including generation, exchange, storage, use, revocation, and replacement of the keys.

A secure system should provide several assurances, such as confidentiality, integrity, and availability of data as well as authenticity and non-repudiation. When used correctly, crypto helps to give these assurances. Cryptography can ensure the confidentiality and integrity of data in transit and at rest. It can also authenticate senders and recipients to one another and protect against repudiation.

Software systems often have multiple endpoints, typically multiple clients, and one or more back-end servers. These client/server communications occur over networks that cannot be trusted. Contact occurs over open, public networks such as the Internet, or private networks, which external attackers or malicious insiders may compromise.

It can protect communications that traverse untrusted networks. An adversary may attempt to carry out two main types of attacks on a network. Passive attacks involve an attacker simply listening to a network segment and trying to read sensitive information as it travels. Passive attacks may be online (in which an attacker reads traffic in real-time) or offline (in which an attacker captures traffic in real-time and views it later—perhaps after spending some time decrypting it). Active attacks involve an attacker impersonating a client or server, intercepting communications in transit, and viewing and modifying the contents before passing them on to their intended destination (or dropping them entirely).

The confidentiality and integrity protections offered by cryptographic protocols such as SSL/TLS can protect communications from malicious eavesdropping and tampering. Authenticity protections ensure that users are communicating with the systems as intended. For example, are you sending your online banking password to your bank or someone else?

It can also be used to protect data at rest. Data on a removable disk or database can be encrypted to prevent disclosing sensitive data should the physical media be lost or stolen. In addition, it can also provide integrity protection of data at rest to detect malicious tampering.

Different Types of Cryptography

Numerous cryptographic algorithms are in use, but in general, they can be broken into three categories: secret key cryptography, public key cryptography, and hash functions. Each has its role to play within the cryptographic landscape.

Secret key cryptography: The Caesar cipher discussed above is an excellent example of private key cryptography. In the model we used, if encrypted messages were being exchanged between Caesar and one of his centurions, both parties would have to know the key — in this case, how many letters forward or backward in the alphabet you need to move to transform plaintext to ciphertext or vice versa. But the essential needs to stay a secret between the two of them. You couldn't send the key along with the message, for instance, because if both fell into enemy hands, the message would be straightforward for them to decipher, defeating the whole purpose of encrypting it in the first place. Caesar and his centurion would presumably have to discuss the key when they saw each other in person, though this is less than ideal when wars are being fought over long distances.

Secret key cryptography, sometimes a symmetric key, is widely used to keep data confidential. It can be beneficial for maintaining a local hard drive private; for instance, since the same user generally encrypts and decrypts the protected data, sharing the secret key is not an issue. Secret key cryptography can also be used to keep messages transmitted across the internet confidential; however, to successfully make this happen, you need to deploy our following form of cryptography in tandem with it.

Public key cryptography: Caesar may have been able to confer with his centurions in person, but you don't want to go into your bank and talk to the teller to learn what the private key is for encrypting your electronic communication with the bank — that would defeat the purpose of online banking. In general, to function securely, the internet needs a way for communicating parties to establish a secure communications channel while only talking to each other across an inherently insecure network. The way this works is via public key cryptography.

Each participant has two keys in public key cryptography, sometimes called an asymmetric key. One is shared and sent to anyone the party wishes to communicate with. That's the key used to encrypt messages. But the other key is private, shared with nobody, and it's necessary to decrypt those messages. To use a metaphor: think of the public key as opening a slot in a mailbox just wide enough to drop a letter in. Give those dimensions to anyone you feel might send you a letter. The private key is what you use to open the mailbox so you can get the letters out.

The mathematics of how you can use one key to encrypt a message and another to decrypt it is much less intuitive than how the key to the Caesar cipher works. The Infosec Institute has a deep dive if you're interested. The core principle that makes the process work is that the two keys are related mathematically, so it's easy to derive the public key from the private key but not vice versa. For instance, the private key might be two huge prime numbers, which you'd multiply to get the public key.

The computations needed for public key cryptography are much more complex and resource intensive than those behind secret critical infrastructure. Fortunately, you don't need to use it to protect every message you send online. Instead, what usually happens is that one party will use public key cryptography to encrypt a message containing yet another cryptographic key. Having been safely transmitted across the insecure internet, this key will become the private key that encodes a much longer communications session encrypted via secret key encryption.

In this way, public key cryptography assists the cause of confidentiality. But these public keys are also part of a more extensive set of functions known as public critical infrastructure, or PKI. PKI provides ways to be sure that any public key is associated with a specific person or institution. A message encrypted with a public key thus confirms the identity of the sender, establishing authentication and non-repudiation.

Hash functions: Public and private key cryptographic algorithms transform plaintext into ciphertext and back into plaintext. By contrast, a hash function is a one-way encryption algorithm: once you've encrypted your plaintext, you can't recover it from the resulting ciphertext (a hash).

This might make hash functions seem like a somewhat pointless exercise. But the key to their usefulness is that no two plaintexts will produce the same hash for any given hash function. (Mathematically, this needs to be corrected, but for any hash function in use, the chances of it happening are generally vanishingly small and can be safely ignored.)

This makes hashing algorithms an excellent tool for ensuring data integrity. For instance, a message can be sent along with its hash. Upon receiving the message, you can run the same hashing algorithm on the text; if the hash you produce differs from the one accompanying the news, you know the message has been modified in transit.

Hashing is also used to ensure the confidentiality of passwords. Storing passwords as plaintext is a big security no-no because that makes users prone to account and identity theft in the wake of data breaches (which sadly doesn't stop big players from doing it). If, instead, you store a hashed version of a user's password, hackers won't be able to decrypt it and use it elsewhere, even if they do manage to breach your defenses. When a legitimate user logs in with their password, you can hash it and check against the hash you have on file.

Cryptography and Crypto

A large draw of cryptocurrencies is their security and transparency on the blockchain. All of that relies on cryptographic mechanisms. That is how most blockchain-based cryptocurrencies maintain security; therefore, it constitutes the very nature of cryptocurrencies.

It was on a cryptography message board back in 2009 that Bitcoin creator Satoshi Nakamoto suggested a way to solve the double-spend problem that had long been the Achilles heel of digital currencies. The double-spend problem occurs when the same crypto unit has the potential to be spent twice, which would destroy trust in them as an online payment solution and make them essentially worthless.

Nakamoto proposed using a peer-to-peer distributed ledger that was timestamped and secured cryptographically. That led to the creation of the blockchain as we know it today. As with all technology, cryptography will evolve to keep up with the demands of a secure digital environment. This is especially true with the growing adoption of blockchains and cryptocurrencies across industries and borders.

Ethereum & Cardano

Ethereum

Ethereum is a blockchain platform with its cryptocurrency, called Ether (ETH) or Ethereum, and its programming language, Solidity.

As a blockchain network, Ethereum is a decentralized public ledger for verifying and recording transactions. The network's users can create, publish, monetize, and use applications on the platform, using its Ether cryptocurrency as payment. Insiders call the decentralized applications on the network "dApps."

Ethereum was created to enable developers to build and publish intelligent contracts and distributed applications that can be used without the risks of downtime, fraud, or interference from a third party.

Ethereum describes itself as "the world's programmable blockchain." It distinguishes itself from Bitcoin as a programmable network that serves as a marketplace for financial services, games, and apps, all of which can be paid for in Ether cryptocurrency and are safe from fraud, theft, or censorship.

Ethereum was launched in July 2015 by a small group of blockchain enthusiasts. They included Joe Lubin, founder of ConsenSys, a blockchain applications developer that uses the

Ethereum network. Another co-founder, Vitalik Buterin, is credited with originating the Ethereum concept and now serves as its CEO and public face. Buterin is sometimes described as the world's youngest crypto billionaire.

The Ether cryptocurrency was designed to be used within the Ethereum network. However, like Bitcoin, Ether is now an accepted form of payment by some merchants and service vendors. Overstock, Shopify, and CheapAir are online sites accepting Ether as payment.

The founders of Ethereum were among the first to consider the potential of blockchain technology for uses beyond the secure trading of virtual currency. Its ETH cryptocurrency was created primarily as a payment medium for apps built on its platform.

Its invulnerability to hackers and other snoopers has opened up possibilities for storing private information, from healthcare records to voting systems. Its reliance on cryptocurrency opened up opportunities for programmers to create and market games and business applications on the network.

A blockchain may be invulnerable to hacker attacks, but it's not for lack of trying. In 2016, a malicious actor stole over $50 million worth of Ether that had been raised for a project called The DAO, a set of smart contracts created by a third party and originating from Ethereum's software platform. The successful raid was blamed on a third-party developer.

The Ethereum community opted to reverse the theft by creating a "hard fork," invalidating the existing blockchain and creating a second Ethereum blockchain. The original is known as Ethereum Classic.

As of May 2021, Ethereum was the second-largest virtual currency on the market, behind only Bitcoin. The number of ETHs in circulation crossed the 100 million mark in 2018.

Unlike Bitcoin, there is no limit to the number of ETHs that can be created.

Ethereum is currently undergoing a long-awaited upgrade known as Ethereum 2.0, which is intended to allow the network to scale up while addressing congestion problems that have slowed it down in the past.

How would you explain Ethereum to someone in the simplest of terms? It's relatively easy. Ethereum, like any blockchain, is a database of information designed to be unhackable. Ether, or ETH, is the cryptocurrency used to complete transactions on the blockchain.

Unlike in a traditional database, information in a blockchain is organized as a chronological "chain" made up of "blocks" of data. For instance, every Ether coin transaction must be verified and recorded as an additional block on that coin's unique blockchain. This process of recording every transaction in a sequence is why a blockchain is often compared to a ledger.

The Ethereum blockchain stores more than transaction records for Ether currency. It allows software developers to create games and business applications, called dApps, and market them to users. Those users want to take advantage of the relative lack of risks that come with storing sensitive information on the World Wide Web.

But is it better than Bitcoin and its competitors? In some ways, it is. Unlike the Bitcoin blockchain, Ethereum was not created to support a cryptocurrency. The Ether cryptocurrency was created to provide an in-house currency for applications built on the Ethereum blockchain.

In other words, Ethereum has broader ambitions. It wants to be a platform for all applications that can safely store information. Despite their differences, the two are the creators of virtual currencies that have become rivals in the investing world. And virtual currencies are just that: They are coins that have no physical existence but are represented by a string of codes that can be exchanged at a price agreed upon by a buyer and a seller. And what's next for Ethereum? It's worth noting that Ethereum has been met with healthy skepticism. For one, Ethereum is far from scalable, meaning it can't support many users right now, throwing a wrench in the idea of a "world computer" that disrupts Google, Facebook, and other centralized platforms.

Ethereum 2.0, launched Dec. 1, 2020, aims to fix some of these issues. Other scaling technologies, such as Raiden – which has been in the works for years – could also help with the scalability problem.

Cardano

Cardano is a third-generation, decentralized proof-of-stake (PoS) blockchain platform designed to be a more efficient alternative to proof-of-work (PoW) networks. The infrastructure burden of growing costs, energy use, and slow transaction times limit scalability, interoperability, and sustainability on PoW networks like Ethereum.

Charles Hoskinson, the co-founder of the proof-of-work (PoW) blockchain Ethereum, understood the implications of these challenges to blockchain networks and began developing Cardano and its primary cryptocurrency, named ada, in 2015, launching the platform and the ADA token in 2017.

The Cardano platform runs on the Ouroboros consensus protocol. Ouroboros, created by Cardano in its foundation phase, is the first PoS protocol that not only was proved to be secure but also was the first to be informed by scholarly academic research. Each development phase, or era, in the Cardano roadmap is anchored by the research-based framework, incorporating peer-reviewed insights with evidence-based methods to progress toward and achieve the milestones related to the future directions of the use applications of the blockchain network and the ADA token.

Some back story on Cardano and its origins and purpose. It is closely related to Ethereum, and its separation shows how divided the cryptocurrency market and industry can become.

Charles Hoskinson started Cardano with his former Ethereum colleague Jerry Wood in 2014 after leaving Ethereum, following a difference in opinion with the team running the Ethereum Foundation over governance and the role of venture capital. In the early days of Ethereum, Hoskinson saw the need for a more standardized and scalable blockchain. With his mathematics background, Hoskinson began thinking about more scientific ways to build a blockchain. During this time, Hoskinson connected with Jeremy Wood, a former Ethereum co-worker looking to create a better blockchain and smart contracts platform. The two began to pursue Cardano as it exists today.

Cardano is supported by the same-named foundation that aids the research and development of the protocol and its community. The Cardano project's development is spearheaded by the for-profit company Input Output Hong Kong, also called IOHK. It comes as no surprise that Hoskinson also heads IOHK. The project signed up leading academics in several universities worldwide to review their work before announcing Cardano. It was peer-tested and approved and crafted with functionality and a democratic aspect heavily built into it. From the beginning, Hoskinson wanted Cardano to be community-driven because he knew that would keep it strong and viable throughout the years. A strong base of users who truly believed in the system would go a long way to keep it alive, healthy, and safe.

2017 Cardano launched its native cryptocurrency ADA after famous and celebrated 19th-century mathematician Ada Lovelace. Lovelace is credited as being one of the world's first computer programmers by being the first to publish her idea of a machine algorithm for a computer-like "analytical engine." The Cardano project itself is named after the Italian polymath Gerolamo Cardano. The homages to Lovelace and Cardano are just other examples of the team behind this promising blockchain and altcoin tipping their hats to those who came before them and made the entire project and system possible.

Cardano's main applications are in identity management and traceability. The former application can be used to streamline and simplify processes that require the collection of data from multiple sources. The latter application can track and audit a product's manufacturing processes from provenance to finished goods and, potentially, eliminate the market for counterfeit goods.

Oversight of the advancement of the Cardano protocol ecosystem is decentralized, and Cardano's partners share responsibilities: The Cardano Foundation, IOHK, and EMURGO. The Cardano Foundation, a not-for-profit organization, is the legal custodian responsible for the primary oversight and supervision of the Cardano brand. The foundation advances the visibility of the protocol on the global stage, cultivates use-case opportunities, and connects with policymakers, regulators, and academia.

IOHK is the software engineering and technology company responsible for building Cardano, with a research arm dedicated to promoting blockchain education. IOHK works closely with academic partners to not only further its educational mission but also improve the long-term scalability of the Cardano protocol by using the most recent peer-reviewed scientific research to inform platform updates before implementation. EMURGO is the global technology partner responsible for driving the commercial adoption of the Cardano protocol, integrating businesses across a wide range of sectors into their blockchain system.

The organizations behind Cardano have released three products: Atala PRISM, Atala SCAN, and Atala Trace. The first product is marketed as an identity management tool that can provide access to services. For example, it can be used to verify credentials to open a bank account or eligibility for government aid. The other two products trace a product's journey through a supply chain.

Cardano is also developing an innovative contract platform that will be stable and secure for developing enterprise-level decentralized apps. Shortly, the team at Cardano plans to use a democratic on-chain governance system called Project Catalyst to manage the development and execution of projects. They will also revamp their treasury management system to fund future costs using Project Catalyst.

The Cardano blockchain is stratified into the Cardano Settlement Layer (CSL) and the Cardano Computational Layer (CCL), which separates Cardano from the regular innovative contract platform. Ethereum runs a single-layer architecture, which has seen it experience network congestion, slow transaction speed, and high gas fees.

Cardano seeks to address these issues through the CSL and CCL. Its CSL layer facilitates peer-to-peer transactions such as tokens transfer between users. The CSL is Cardano's balance ledger. Using a proof-of-stake consensus algorithm (Ouroboros protocol) to generate new blocks and confirm transactions, Cardano wants to improve Bitcoin's proof-of-work protocol.

The CCL layer is where Cardano truly distinguishes itself. The CCL powers the computational needs of the blockchain, enabling the execution of smart contracts.

This layer is operated separately from the settlement layer to afford flexibility if the need for changes arises. Its off-chain protocol offers greater data storage flexibility and an access model that lets users create customized rules when validating transactions.

High fees have been a limiting factor for the DeFi space. As the appeal for these projects increases with record values locked up, Ethereum's gas fees have made them an expensive endeavor. Cardano is aiming to fix this and more with its Mary upgrade.

Cardano developers can now create custom tokens or import projects from other blockchains into the Cardano network. This could benefit exciting projects like the DeFi and NFT ecosystems.

Will Cardano's Mary upgrade finally position the one-time underdog as a serious challenger to Ethereum? While Cardano is innovating, other blockchain platforms — including Ethereum — are in a race to work out issues like scalability and sustainability.

But in the world of technology, it's not necessarily the best technology that wins, but the one with the better business strategy. Time will tell whether Cardano's Africa and Fortune 500 strategy will prevail.

What about Cardano has raised the level of interest in popularity around it? On its surface, it appears much like many other altcoins on the market. It has a volatile nature and its fair share of ups and downs; it can be traded on many online exchanges, just like Ethereum and plenty of other coins that rival and try to challenge Bitcoin. So what is it that makes Cardano so unique? Its name recognition, the people behind it, and the science and technology that drives Cardano are the main features that should draw investors to it. Just because it was assembled and launched by the same people who got Ethereum up and running is a significant draw for many. Then the blockchain technology that runs Cardano is just icing on the cake of these promising altcoins.

But there are drawbacks, too, things to consider when you put your money into Cardano. Firstly, its system and technique, and functionality are limited. Cardano is indeed built upon an open-source blockchain that can be adapted and improved by others in the community. That is a vital feature, a huge benefit that makes Cardano even more attractive. However, it is also hard to master and isn't the most accessible technology to adapt to enterprises and businesses. It takes much work and is challenging for new programmers. The nuts and bolts that run

Cardano are complicated, complex and have a steep learning curve. It is unlikely that you won't see the Cardano system in many businesses and other altcoins soon because it is challenging to master, even though it is open to anyone who wants to take a shot at it.

Still, despite its drawbacks, Cardano is one of the most promising altcoins. There is a reason so many people are putting their money into Cardano, and it's more than just the team behind it. Cardano has a back-end functionality that is strong, cutting-edge, and can improve and grow. Plus, the community that buys into Cardano is the same community that runs, changes, adjusts, and benefits from it. Many people are drawn to cryptocurrency because of the feeling of society that can come with it. Cardano has a strong community feel to it, and that is just one of the significant reasons why it has proven to be resilient and enticing again and again and again.

Chapter 5: Altcoins

You have now learned about cryptocurrency generally and its most popular and well-known offspring: Bitcoin. Indeed, when people talk about crypto, they are almost always going to mention Bitcoin because it is the coin that has taken the world by storm and shown even the most stubborn naysayers that there is potential in cryptocurrencies of all types.

In the beginning, there was only Bitcoin. It was the only form of cryptocurrency that people cared to have. But, over time, the crypto world has evolved, and what was once only one has now become hundreds upon hundreds. There are countless ways to invest in cryptocurrency; you do not have to be beholden to solely Bitcoin.

What are these other forms of cryptocurrency? They are called altcoins - and they are plenty. But what are they? How do they work? Why do they exist? Let's dive in.

Why Do Altcoins Exist?

Altcoins are an alternative to Bitcoin and exist to expand the field of cryptocurrency and allow investors and buyers more options when they are looking to enter the booming marketplace of crypto. That is why altcoins exist and the most polite way of saying it. There are other reasons why altcoins have come to be - and even more reasons why they have become so popular.

Essentially, altcoins were made because there is an opportunity for others to experience financial growth. The concept behind all cryptocurrency is that people can buy and sell goods and pay for them with a new form of digital payment. That is very much the truth. However, there are other reasons why cryptocurrency has become so popular. For one, it is an investment opportunity, a way for people to put money into the market and ride the following success. If you play your cards right, you can invest several hundred dollars into cryptocurrencies and walk away with thousands. This is exciting for many people. The businesses and entrepreneurs who started altcoins all over the world saw a chance to make money, much money. They knew that if they got in on the ground floor and offered something that stood a chance of making a lot of financial gains for many, they would find fans and people willing to accept the opportunity to turn a profit.

Yes, altcoins exist so people can make money. There is no shame in that fact. However, why don't people invest in Bitcoin, especially since it has proven to be the most popular and successful form of crypto? For one, these people think that there is a chance that the altcoin they are starting or buying into can become the next big thing, a cryptocurrency that threatens Bitcoin's place at the top of the food chain. There is always room for expansion and success in cryptocurrency; who is to say the next altcoin might not be the biggest yet?

Additionally, many people look to altcoins because they may feature something that Bitcoin does not. For example, because of the processing it goes through, it takes time to spend or receive Bitcoin successfully. The coin needs to be sent; it must go through the entire crypto-mining process, verifying that everything is accurate and legitimate. This takes much longer than it takes to slide a debit card through a machine at a local business. Certain altcoins, however, have sped up the process. With specific altcoins on the market, you can make a purchase and have it paid for quickly. That is a massive benefit to some of these coins and a significant reason why some people are drawn to them. There is also the fact that some altcoins are even more anonymous than Bitcoin. While most of the people buying things with cryptocurrency are entirely above the board and not doing anything scandalous or criminal, some people are using crypto pay for illegal goods and services. Why not use an altcoin that cannot track your identity or location? Some altcoins appeal to people for that very reason alone.

Altcoins exist because the world of cryptocurrency is a booming marketplace full of many potential buyers, investors, inventors, and more. It is an area of industry that is looking to expand continually, and there are people from all over the world looking to get into that. They are searching for alternatives, the next breakthrough, or just a chance for them to make some money. That is why altcoins exist. The potential in the cryptocurrency world is so vast and endless that altcoins began to capitalize on that.

While the field of altcoins is now crowded and still constantly growing, it is sometimes different. There was a time when there was just one single altcoin to compete against Bitcoin. Even though, back then, it wasn't much of a competition at all.

The first altcoin was an experiment, a quest to see if the possible idea of altcoins was even possible or if it was just a hope and a dream that would never get off the ground. However, like cryptocurrency, altcoins eventually grew stronger and became an entire industry rivaling Bitcoin's popularity and potential growth.

The world of altcoins began in 2010, just a couple of years after Bitcoin was up and running. On the BitcoinTalk forums, a discussion about Bitcoin and cryptocurrency was in full swing. From these conversations about alternative cryptocurrencies and what they could achieve, Namecoin was born. It was the first altcoin, and, like Bitcoin itself, it was more than just a cryptocurrency. With Namecoin, the construction and functionality were tied to a decentralized DNS system. It was a complicated system, but the Namecoin system would have value in multiple ways, both by acting as a currency and as being tied to domain name creation.

When a Namecoin block is created, it is tied to a unique domain name that can be sold for money. Therefore, each coin has a monetary value but also has value because it is related to a domain name, which can also raise money for the owner.

In almost every way, Namecoin is a Bitcoin clone. It was so closely related to Bitcoin that Bitcoin miners could also mine Namecoin simultaneously. This method, called pooled mining, was another significant feature that invited and impressed many. Namecoin was the first, but it only lasted for a while. Over time, Namecoin eventually faded and is now seen as a dead coin. However, its place in altcoin history was solidified long ago. Namecoin proved to millions that alternative currencies were possible, had potential, and could carry promise and purpose that stood on their own and were separate from Bitcoin. This was a significant moment in cryptocurrency history, the start of something massive.

The floodgates began to open after Namecoin. Other industries and creators began to craft their altcoins. Before investors knew it, the marketplace became increasingly filled with altcoins with different names, features, premises, and promises. Online exchanges started offering these altcoins, allowing users to invest, buy, and trade them just like with Bitcoin. None of these new coins would ever truly rival and surpass Bitcoin in terms of popularity and value, but they all made splashes in their ways.

One of the most attractive features of altcoins is the variety. Nowadays, there are indeed hundreds of altcoins for investors to choose from. This means there are many chances at finding the next big thing, some altcoin that floats right below the surface, looking to break big. An intelligent investor can do much research and digging and find something others have yet to notice.

A true investor will study the marketplace and find the altcoins that have the most potential and the most significant chance to make an impact. Someone who knows how the market works, what it wants, and what it reacts to will be able to decipher the wills and desires of the market. That way, they will know what altcoins will speak to investors and which have the most excellent chance of breaking through. Like all things cryptocurrency, the more knowledge you have, the more power you have.

Some people want to invest solely in Bitcoin when they enter cryptocurrency. They feel that Bitcoin is the only sure thing, an investment that will always pay off and has fewer risks than others. As stated before, countless people think that Bitcoin is the only cryptocurrency. Is that short-sighted? It sure is, but it's better for you in many ways. The fewer people seeking out altcoins, the better chance you have to be the one who stumbles upon the next altcoin that will create waves.

A limited view of the crypto market is all well and good for some people, but if you are looking to become a talented and successful trader, you should fill your portfolio with some altcoins. Why? Because altcoins give you more opportunities for success, variety, and potential. It's a simple investment approach that you would be taught in any investing class: the wider variety of cryptocurrencies you own, the bigger your chances for success. With more options, you have more possibilities for financial success. Why would you limit yourself only to Bitcoin? Yes, you could make your fortune with only Bitcoin; it limits you significantly. Ideally, you should find altcoins with great potential and study and understand them and the market. Once you comprehend how the cryptocurrency market functions and why it encounters its usual ups and downs, you will better handle which altcoins show promise, which could become hits, and which ones will become misses.

Altcoins are a terrific way to make more money and find options for success that others may have missed. But it would be best always to choose the altcoins you want to invest in. Instead, it would be best to make your choices based on understanding the market and the history of cryptocurrency, Bitcoin, and altcoins. Know what has driven other altcoins to great heights - and deep lows. You will begin to see patterns in the cryptocurrency world, certain features that appeal to investors and those that don't. This will inform your choices and lead you to find the right altcoin. With so many options out there and so many chances for great value and significant loss, it is essential that you take buying altcoin very seriously. Otherwise, it is just like you throwing your money away.

Investing in altcoins is a way to open up more possibilities to yourself and also a way to indeed be in touch with the nature and personality of the cryptocurrency landscape. There have been many altcoins over the years, and many more still to this day, and each of them has the potential to be something that could break the system wide open, rival Bitcoin in a major way, and create a significant financial windfall for investors. There is no reason to ignore altcoins. Not giving them proper attention is a surefire way to miss out on the chance to become an investor that others envy.

The Most Common Altcoins

While you may know about altcoins, how many are there? Did you know that there are not just dozens of options for you when investing in altcoins but hundreds, even thousands, of ways to spend and make money?

It's true; the world of altcoins has exploded over the last few years. Bitcoin is no longer alone, not by a long shot. Now plenty of cryptocurrency investors still need to buy into Bitcoin. Instead, they choose to find an altcoin that seems appealing to them. Certain businesses are also beginning to create their altcoins, sure they could create something powerful, modern, and cutting-edge.

There are so many altcoins out there that the thought of finding the one that is right for you is downright overwhelming. While you could spend days researching and looking into altcoins to find the one you want to invest in, it is best to know the top names in the game and the most significant coins that have made the biggest splashes. You have many more options than these, but here are some of the most impressive, robust, and reliable altcoins that have significantly changed the cryptocurrency world.

Litecoin

If we talk about altcoins, we might as well start by discussing the one that has created the most significant impact. Litecoin is not just a big altcoin, it is a vast altcoin, and many people feel that it has now surpassed Bitcoin in terms of power and potential. If anyone can take down Bitcoin as the most significant crypto in the world, it is undoubtedly Litecoin.

Created in 2011, Litecoin has quickly become the gold standard of altcoins. There is no doubt or question that Litecoin is the top of the top and the highest-rated and most sought-after altcoin on the market. Its popularity and success have steadily gained and, most impressively, stayed stable throughout its lifetime. In a marketplace that sees a lot of volatility and sudden change, Litecoin has remained consistent and strong over the years. This sort of consistency appeals to many buyers, especially new ones, and that only makes the Litecoin fanbase grow in size year after year.

Like all altcoins, Litecoin doesn't cost as much as Bitcoin. That is just one of the many benefits of it, one of the many reasons Litecoin continues to bring in new investors, even people who have yet to buy a slice of Bitcoin. You do not have to lose as much money when investing in Litecoin. However, other features make this altcoin attractive to all investors. The amount of Litecoin that exists - or will exist - is also incredibly appealing. Regarding availability and the future of Litecoin, there are just so many more Litecoins to mine. That is surprising since Litecoin is much like Bitcoin and wants a manageable supply. This altcoin was started as a branch of Bitcoin initially. It now has a supply limit of about 84 million, which is far more than the limit Bitcoin will have. That means there is more of a supply of Litecoin, which means you have a better chance at buying cheaper because the demand doesn't affect supply as much as other altcoins, especially with Bitcoin. Some consider Litecoin the best altcoin to look into when starting your investing career.

Ethereum

Whenever you mention Litecoin as the gold standard for altcoins, you must say Ethereum, the silver to Litecoin's gold. It may not be *as* popular as Litecoin, but it still has a large, loyal fanbase that sings its praises often.

This altcoin has grown in popularity over the years and has shown how devoted it is to the future of all cryptocurrencies. In 2016, Ethereum split into two: Ethereum and Ethereum Classic. The price of Ethereum is relatively low compared to Bitcoin and some other altcoins, but many predict its value will only go up and up.

The most promising aspect of Ethereum is its speed. While it can take around 15 minutes for a Bitcoin to be encrypted, mined, and cleared, it only takes about 15 seconds for the same to be done with Ethereum. That isn't just fast; it is *blazingly* fast. The speed is excellent; the price isn't as lovely. It will cost you a pretty penny to invest in Ethereum. But it has such promise and growth ahead that you would be silly to write off Ethereum. For serious investors, those who don't mind throwing down a large chunk of change on the promise of more, Ethereum is the way to go.

Bitcoin Cash

The name for this altcoin confuses many. Bitcoin Cash? So this is a form of Bitcoin? If that is the case, why don't people buy Bitcoin?

We understand the confusion and know an explanation is needed.

Bitcoin Cash is one of the earliest altcoins on the market and holds the distinction of being an oft-publicized hard fork from the original Bitcoin. A fork is when developers and miners cannot see eye-to-eye, and the decision is made to create vast differences in the code and branch off and complete a brand-new form of crypto.

When this happens, the original blockchain continues, and the new cryptocurrency and its chain "fork" off and go their own way. That is what happened with Bitcoin Cash, or BCH. In August 2017, it was created and took off on its own. Since then, it has not proven successful in its own and some people refer to it as Bitcoin Trash. However, its name and affiliation with Bitcoin have led to some confusion.

Cat

This 2023 Pro-Crypto Education, Adoption, and Public Awareness Token will revolutionize cryptocurrencies. Crypto

Adoption Token's (CAT) unique advertising campaigns promote Crypto's immense potential. Join CAT's future! Join a thriving community of forward-thinking people who want to share cryptocurrency's benefits. We can change money and create a better future. These astonishing coins will transform political fundraising. These coins are improving the future by supporting pro-crypto politicians and regulatory reforms. Join the movement and change now! A revolutionary Bitcoin education and advocacy project. A new lobbying business will empower the next generation with strategic crypto knowledge. Introducing a unique project to popularize cryptocurrencies! CAT will empower people with crypto knowledge by making it widely accessible to the public. Adoption coins are changing how people view and participate in this exciting digital frontier through schools, libraries, independent lectures, seminars, and other engaging venues. Join us on this thrilling trip to unveil crypto's secrets and create a better, more informed future!

Celsius

Back in 2018, the Celsius Network earned $20 million via crowdfunding. That shows just how interested people were in Celsius before it officially launched. Since its creation and release, it has written over $6 million in loans and generated more than $11 million in interest.

The fact that Celsius has generated so much money in loans is surprising and encouraging and causes concern. We have seen numerous loaning giants fold over the years because of bad investments and loans that must be paid back. Celsius is too new to the loaning world and will make bad beds and offer loans to people who do not and should not get them. If that is the case, you can expect Celsius to face severe problems in the years ahead. However, there is a chance that Celsius will only continue to expand instead of collapse. And if you are still in Crypto, you know that Celsius has gone bankrupt, and clients with collateral stuck on the failed platform had to look to the bankruptcy courts and process for relief. And now we have another crypto technology with a fun name and yet another crypto that happened to be started by one of the creators behind Ethereum.

Polkadot.

It is fun to say, that's for sure. But Polkadot is far more than just a fun, playful name. It is a technology and system that wants to bring all sorts of other blockchains together for the better of all blockchains and all cryptocurrencies.

At its course, Polkadot is best described as a multi-chain network connecting different specialized blockchains into one unified network. These connected blockchains are called "para chains." These para chains come together to create a network that is uniform, easy to understand, easy to fix and tweak and further evolves. All of the para chains also run independently and parallel to one another. This is good because it prevents a network overload and lets each para chain run quickly and safely while still connected to the entire Polkadot network. Polkadot also created protocols allowing its network to interact with other blockchains. Since its blockchain network is flexible, it has an increased ability to pivot and serve more specific needs.

Why is this so important? What about Polkadot's revolutionary chain of blockchains makes it unique and worthy of your time and money? Its importance comes from Polkadot's ability to create a way for all developers to build blockchains with value, security, and a uniform system.

With Polkadot, blockchains can connect in the para chains. When placed together, these para chains create a so-called "relay chain" in which all transaction addresses are checked and verified, and all data is standardized to understand each system in the relay chain. Polkadot turns all blockchains into one extra-long, extra-safe blockchain.

But there is more to Polkadot than just its blockchain technology. Like Cardano and other cryptocurrency systems, Polkadot offers its coin, predictably named DOT. DOT is an internal cryptocurrency token that can directly influence the Polkadot network. Users who buy into DOT can vote on potential changes within Polkadot, meaning each purchased pass is also a vote and part of the democratic Polkadot process. Polkadot is the creation of cryptocurrency mastermind Gavin Wood, an important figure in the history of rival coins, Ethereum. Wood was co-founder and one of the core developers of Ethereum, which would become one of the biggest names in the game and still proves to be one of the most popular coins in the marketplace. Wood was the man who coded the platform's first implementation, wrote its formal specification, and invented the Solidity contract programming language. He had long ago proven his worth and ability, giving crypto investors plenty of reasons to believe in him and follow his lead.

He moved on from Ethereum, and people were interested in what he would do next. He was satisfied with Polkadot's twist on blockchains and the idea behind connecting them into one giant, extra-safe chain.

On January 11, 2016, Wood moved on from Ethereum entirely and focused all his attention on Polkadot. In Wood's opinion, the new tech that would later be known as Polkadot would deliver on many of the promises that Ethereum still needs to achieve. He had high hopes and many goals in his mind. Wood has said that the original idea for Polkadot popped into his mind in the summer of 2016. Spurred on by fellow developer Marek

Kotewicz, Wood began designing a sharded version of Ethereum that was as simple as possible. By October 2016, Wood had finished the first draft of the Polkadot White Paper, and he immediately knew he had something special.

Since launching on the market, Polkadot has hit many milestones, proving that many people did believe in Wood and followed him onto his new venture. It climbed to become the fourth largest cryptocurrency and achieved a peak market point of $18 billion.

It isn't just investors who believe in Polkadot. Other cryptocurrency companies and teams genuinely believe in the ideas and concepts behind Polkadot too. How is that known? Simply because there are now over 340 projects that are actively being developed on the Polkadot system. All of them will be connected via Polkadot's parchhain system. If so many people who create cryptocurrencies believe in Polkadot, it's no surprise that regular, everyday investors believe in it too.

Why Altcoins?

Some people want to invest solely in Bitcoin when they enter cryptocurrency. They feel that Bitcoin is the only sure thing, an investment that will always pay off and has fewer risks than others.

That's all good for those people, but you should fill your portfolio with some altcoins to become a talented and successful trader. Why? Because altcoins give you more opportunities for success, variety, and potential. Think of it this way: the wider variety of cryptocurrencies you own, the bigger your chances for success. Why limit yourself only to Bitcoin? While you could make your fortune with Bitcoin, it limits you significantly. Instead, you should study altcoins with great potential and research them and the market. Once you understand how the cryptocurrency market works and why it encounters the ups and downs it does, you will have a better handle on which altcoins show promise, which ones could become hits, and which ones will become misses.

Altcoins are a terrific way to make more money and find options for success that others may have missed. But it would be best always to choose the altcoins you want to invest in. Instead, it would be best to make your choices based on understanding the market and the history of cryptocurrency, Bitcoin, and altcoins. Know what has driven other altcoins to great heights - and deep lows. You will begin to see patterns in the cryptocurrency world, certain features that appeal to investors and those that don't. This will inform your choices and lead you to find the right altcoin. With so many options out there and so many chances for great value and significant loss, it is essential that you take buying altcoin very seriously. Otherwise, it is just like you throwing your money away.

How To Buy Bitcoin and Altcoin

Armed with more knowledge about how the market works the way it does, it is time to move onto another vital subject: just where on Earth do you buy crypto and start your trading career? Thankfully, now you have quite a few options. In the early days of crypto, buying some was a challenging task. People needed to learn how to buy their share of cryptocurrency. Mainly because there were no rules or regulations, no set of guidance that told people where to go, how to buy, and what to look for. Remember, everything was created by people who wanted the system and longed for cryptocurrency for ages. They were both the ones dictating how the system worked and were also the ones using it.

In the early days, it was like many people wandering around in a pitch-black room looking for a light switch. They didn't know where to go, they didn't know what to do, and they didn't know the proper steps to take. Over time, a formal procedure began to formulate, and certain websites and message boards emerged. As cryptocurrency became more popular, even with a relatively small group of people, things became much more straightforward. The early days of crypto found people buying and selling coins on message boards, a primitive and complicated approach to trading that took too much time and effort and was far too confusing.

Boy, how times have changed. Today, you can buy cryptocurrency easily. It's as simple as logging into a website. In just a few moments, you can create a brand new account linked to your debit card and be capable of investing in the crypto of your choice.

The websites you can buy cryptocurrency from are called online exchanges, marketplaces for your crypto purchase. Depending on the site, you have specific options when making your purchase. There are many options for you, way more than there used to be even a few years ago. We will get into all these other types of cryptocurrencies, called altcoins, later. However, for our example, we will focus solely on the first and most popular form of cryptocurrency: Bitcoin.

It would be best to decide which online exchange will get your time, energy, and money. This is a crucial decision because a good rule of thumb is to stick with the same online business for all your crypto needs. Whomever you go with, try to stay with them throughout your trading career.

Who do you have to choose from when it comes to online exchanges? The options are varied and always promising. It's up to you to figure out who is your right fit.

Coinbase

Let's start with the biggest name in the game. Coinbase is, without question, the most popular online cryptocurrency exchange globally. It is the most widely-known exchange and is the go-to for many people, the gold standard of cryptocurrency exchanges. For both newcomers and long-term investors, Coinbase has set the bar high for its competitors. Unsurprisingly, Coinbase is investing much money into advertising and recruiting new traders as often as possible. They have made a name for themselves as the premier online exchange.

What attracts so many customers to Coinbase? It's simple, really: they make investing feel like a breeze. The site has proven itself as a safe and easy place to start your Bitcoin investing career. It only charges fees of $.99 to $2.99 depending on the value of your purchase. It also has a wide variety of coins, including some of the best altcoins on the market. Remember, the ability to buy altcoin is one of the most attractive features for some people looking to make their name in the world of cryptocurrency.

Coinbase offers insured wallets for investors. That means if something happens to your investment, Coinbase has you covered - to an extent. That coverage doesn't apply to *all* sorts of mishaps; restrictions apply. However, this is a vital sign that Coinbase takes its customers' satisfaction and safety seriously.

Coinbase also has something called Coinbase Pro, an upgraded version of their system with a different fee structure and more options for data and personalization. Coinbase Pro is another reason this site has become popular and is here to stay. They repeatedly show that they take Bitcoin investing seriously and continually upgrade the customer experience to reflect that.

Binance

Binance was founded in 2017. Since then, it has built an impressive and loyal following of Bitcoin and cryptocurrency investors who have succeeded with this online exchange and sing its praises. Binance is one of the market's most reliable and popular online exchanges. What has caused the explosion of popularity? The fact that this online exchange has a strong emphasis and focus on altcoins is what drives its loyalty among investors. Some say this site is better than even Coinbase if you want to build a portfolio consisting of lesser-known coins. Coinbase has access to 46 different cryptocurrencies, while Binance boasts over 50. That shows just how seriously Binance takes the concept of altcoins.

Binance also prides itself on its selection of essential data and charts. Top-quality analysis is integral to making intelligent investments, and Binance has many data points to help you navigate the market. You can find and make many different graphs with the site, which will help you become an even better crypto trader.

The consumer fees charged at Binance are neither too intense nor weighty. They are usually about .1% of each transaction.

That will encourage new investors to trade and buy without fear and hesitation. It is easy to make a new buy when you are only charged the most minimal amount possible.

It could be better news. There are some things that Binance could improve. For example, the site is built for more advanced users with more experience in the market and using online exchanges. All of the data and analysis take work. It also doesn't work in 22 states in America, which means that if you live in one of those regions, you will be locked out of Binance. However, if you can get your hands on this online exchange and want to experience all that crypto offers - mainly if you invest heavily in altcoins.

KuCoin

Originally hailing from China, KuCoin is one of the most popular online exchanges, which has amassed a significant following with a great offering of cryptocurrencies.

One of the best things about KuCoin, and undoubtedly one of the things that draw in so many of its users, is that it has no deposit fees. And when it comes to the trading fee, it's relatively cheap, too, coming in at just .1%. KuCoin has also committed to having low prices in other aspects too. The withdrawal fees are next to nothing compared to other online exchanges.

But there is more to KuCoin than its cheap fees. It is a site that has a few things that others have done. For one, it offers its very own native cryptocurrency, called KuCoin Shares, also known as KCS. That is an offering you don't find everywhere in the crypto market. Then there is the fact that KuCoin offers many incentives to its users, such as financial rewards when they invite new members onto the site. KuCoin also offers exclusive promotions and bonuses for users actively using the site.

Now, KuCoin also has its downsides too. One of the most significant disadvantages of using the site is that it only works with traditional or fiat currency. That means you must use a different service to get Bitcoin or Ethereum before you can start trading on KuCoin.

KuCoin is an exciting, inventive online exchange for newcomers and seasoned traders. It is thinking outside the box, trying new things, and doing it differently, attempting to give further incentives and rewards that other sites don't offer. All in all, KuCoin will draw people in, and not only because it makes investing and trading coins easy.

eToro

eToro is another wildly popular cryptocurrency online exchange that has now established itself in over 100 countries. Coming out of Israel, eToro started by only offering Bitcoin trading but eventually opened up to accept more forms of crypto, including dozens of promising and below-the-radar altcoins. It now has a vast assortment of options for the most seasoned pro. But even if you're starting in the crypto world, eToro has much to offer you.

Firstly, eToro is an easy-to-use and functional site with many helpful features. These features make investing and trading painless and straightforward, whether you're embarking on your first or one-hundredth trade. The truth is that many online exchanges tend not to be very user-friendly. Sadly, many people have difficulty navigating through investing in crypto, but eToro makes it easy and will leave you feeling like you have a deep and solid understanding of things.

And some of their new ideas are downright brilliant. For example, the copy-trading technique. This stunning feature allows you to replicate the position of other traders in the network, even if you don't know them. That may seem more exciting and original, but it is helpful if you know other people on the site who have found the success you are looking for. Why not just copy their positions? There is no shame in attempting to be like those you respect. If you become a fan of a particular investor or want to mimic their success, the copy-trading feature will let you do just that.

eToro allows you to try your hand at more than just cryptocurrency. You can also buy and trade stocks, currencies, commodities, etc. You will notice that many online exchanges are starting to allow their clients to purchase other things to integrate Bitcoin with supplies and give them a true sense of normalcy.

Gemini

Gemini was started by Tyler and Cameron Winklevoss, the twin brother magnates who claimed they were the ones who created the idea for Facebook. Their foray into the cryptocurrency industry was met with speculation and attention; they had people ready to use Gemini before it fully launched. To some, it felt like a couple of tech start-up celebrities trying to climb aboard the next big thing without truly believing in it. Despite that, the Winklevoss twins put much effort into Gemini to turn it into something special that could stand on its own.

The look and feel of Gemini are slick and modern and look very hip; it makes investing in crypto feel cool. The entire site is incredibly user-friendly, too, and has a lot of intuitive controls that will make it a breeze for first-time users. Great emphasis has been put on creating an easy and painless investing process. Gemini has a lot going for it but has a few downsides. For example, there aren't many currencies to choose from, and the community is still so tight-knit that it may feel small to some. It also might feel a bit too close-knit, a bit too close. That means making many personal connections with others on Gemini is hard. Others claim that Gemini feels sterile and cold, the opposite of inclusive. However, it works well and looks great too, and is accessible in many regions such as the US, Canada, Japan, the UK, and more. As for the aesthetic, that is a look that many other modern sites are going for because it gives off a hip, young, modern vibe.

But that's not all; other ways to purchase Bitcoin and cryptocurrency don't require you to log into a website. As the crypto craze has heated up over the years and all over the globe, a real-world alternative to buying your cryptocurrency has come to life.

Bitcoin ATMS

You may be perplexed by seeing the term "Bitcoin ATM" listed here because it has been told to you again and again that you cannot buy Bitcoins or cryptocurrency in the real world. That is still true; you can't purchase them like any tangible asset. But the times have changed, and you can buy crypto in person. Sort of. Since the creation of Bitcoin ATMs, online exchanges aren't the only way for you to make a Bitcoin purchase. Investing has now become as easy as walking up to an ATM. That is because there are now Bitcoin ATMs in the world. Like a regular bank ATM, a Bitcoin ATM allows you to place your money in exchange for some Bitcoin. But since Bitcoin doesn't physically exist, placing your money in a Bitcoin ATM is like putting your fiat currency online. You will never see it again, but you know it is out there, making you money.

The concept behind Bitcoin ATMs could be more precise because, unlike traditional ATMs, you are not depositing or withdrawing cash at one of these machines. Yes, you are placing money into the machine. But it isn't going into your account. Instead, a Bitcoin ATM is used to buy and sell Bitcoin using fiat currency. So you walk up to the machine, enter your information, deposit your cash, and then choose the cryptocurrency you want to purchase. It is a way to enter the Bitcoin industry and invest without logging into the computer.

Buying or selling with a Bitcoin ATM is relatively simple and resembles the steps taken at a regular, traditional ATM. First, you approach the machine, and the first thing you have to do is verify your identity. Most Bitcoin ATMs will typically ask you to enter your mobile phone information. After entering that, you will be sent a text message to verify your identity before moving forward.

If you want to purchase Bitcoin at an ATM, you must deposit the appropriate amount of cash. After that, the automated teller machine will generate a unique QR code that your digital wallet app will scan on your phone. This way, the ATM tells your digital wallet that the transaction was a success and adds the digital funds to your wallet. Throughout the entire process, no money is ever changed hands aside from the initial deposit made into the machine. This may scare some people off since they need to get used to having an ATM *not* give them something. But this is a Bitcoin ATM, and, like all things cryptocurrency, it heavily emphasizes the Internet. Newcomers must be comfortable that they won't pull money out of the machine, only put it in.

The creation of Bitcoin ATMs shows just how popular cryptocurrency is becoming. Indeed, they wouldn't be installed worldwide if people weren't using them. No, Bitcoin ATMs offer that people are flocking to cryptocurrency, which is becoming increasingly popular and more mainstream. This is a sign of progress, that more people are adapting to cryptocurrency, and that you are getting in at the right time to start your investing career.

The fees these ATMs charge is outrageous and will only make sense for some people. At some point, these Bitcoin ATMs will merge with regular retail establishments. You should be able to go to any CVS and tell them you want to buy X amount of Bitcoin; they will tell you the fiat dollar amount you owe, you pay, and they deposit the amount in crypto to your wallet.

How Do I Store Cryptocurrency?

The safety of buying cryptocurrency was mentioned before, and the conclusion was made that, while it has risks, cryptocurrency is a safe commodity to invest in. The chances of any hacking or thievery stealing away your accumulated wealth are rare. It is rarer than rare. Although, the case is never zero. It could happen.

That is what leads some people to invest in a wallet. What is a wallet? A wallet is exactly what it sounds like a place for you to store your funds. However, since this is a cryptocurrency, a crypto wallet has a significant digital aspect tied to it. How do you keep something that doesn't exist, you may ask yourself? If it is all digital, what does the wallet hold inside it? This is a very stylish digital wallet since this is a modern digital currency.

A cryptocurrency wallet stores private keys that act as your specialized ID, the unique code allowing you to trade your crypto with others. The way that a crypto wallet works is that you gain access to it via a unique password that only you know. As with all passwords, you should never give away your crypto wallet. Otherwise, you open yourself up for severe pain and financial loss.

It is important to note that most online exchanges offer in-house crypto wallets. When you purchase crypto through these sites, they are stored in the area as well, and you can log into the website, monitor your crypto, and send, invest, and buy more directly through the site. This leads many people to ask why to go outside the area you purchased your crypto in. Why not just use the wallet that they provide you? The answer is that many people want extra security for their investments. They want to go above and beyond and buy a wallet that gives them even more safety. Many wallet and ledger companies worldwide have proven themselves to millions of customers, companies that go a step beyond online exchanges and promise more.

There are multiple types of crypto wallets in the marketplace today, all with their benefits and drawbacks. Depending on the type of trader you are, and the kind of safety you desire, there is a wallet that will feel perfect for you. For example, a web wallet, as you imagine, allows you to receive, send, and store your Bitcoin and cryptocurrency directly from a web browser. This basic form of a wallet is easy to use and has a little learning curve. Almost all online exchanges offering an account will also give you a free web wallet. However, it is usually advised that you research and invest in a different type of wallet, one with a few more robust safety measures that will bring you more comfort and security. While online exchanges are a great place to find, buy, and trade crypto, they are not always the best place to go when you want to store it.

There are also desktop wallets, which store your private keys directly onto a hard drive. This keeps all of your money in one central location. A desktop wallet turns your computer into a safe with your hard-earned cryptocurrency. And since it is only stored in that one location, you can only access this wallet if you can access the sole computer with the hard drive. This is a great benefit because you will always know where your money is, giving many users peace of mind. However, you must ensure that the computer you install your desktop wallet on is safer than safe and invulnerable to intrusion by outside parties.

Additionally, there are also mobile wallets as well. They are portable devices that you can take on the go on your smartphones. Using QR codes and other mobile technology, these mobile wallets allow you to access and monitor your funds often and with little work.

Hardware wallets are one of the most common types. They resemble the little USB drives you see in the hands of many students and business people, the little hard drives you can plug into a laptop and carry your information on the go. Like USB drives, the hardware wallet is a physical way to have a non-physical item: your cryptocurrency. With a hardware wallet, you can access your funds via a password only you know. As these hardware wallets become increasingly popular, they become more functional and easier to find and use. They now come with their apps, created specifically for them. The hardware wallet market is growing increasingly and is one of the most exciting industries in all cryptocurrency. It is also one of the safest.

The added security of a password you created for your hardware wallet is one of the many bonuses of owning one. The fact that you can take the wallet offline and disconnect it from the internet makes it safe from hackers, while the password makes it safe from anyone who gets their hands on your wallet. These layers of protection create the hardware wallet even safer, easier to use, and even more reliable.

Chapter 6: Blockchain Beyond Crypto

How is Blockchain Changing the World?

As you can see, blockchain technology is used by many companies in many other industries. It is a giant, global spreadsheet that is accessed by millions of people all over the world. It's open source so that anyone can change the underlying code, and they can see what's going on. It's genuinely peer-to-peer; it doesn't require powerful intermediaries to authenticate or settle transactions.

That idea alone is one of the ways that blockchain is so revolutionary and game-changing. It makes the little man just as powerful as those at the top.

But blockchain will change the world for more than just that. Take sending money, for example. Sending money abroad can take days. At best, this is frustrating; at worst, it could mean friends or family lacking necessities or waiting for emergency medical treatment.

Currently, banks hold foreign currencies in nostro/vostro accounts in other countries and use the SWIFT messaging system to arrange transfers. The transfer is usually done on the same business day if an agreement exists between the two banks. But in developing countries, where currencies are strictly controlled, your bank must use intermediaries or liquidity agents, which is more expensive, time-consuming, and labor-intensive.

Blockchain solutions dramatically reduce the time and cost of sending money abroad. With participating banks connected through a blockchain network, all the compliance and ID checks are fulfilled automatically and authenticated by cryptographic signatures. Once cleared, transactions are usually settled in just a few seconds, leaving an immutable, transparent record for both banks.

What about buying a home? Did you know blockchain will assist that age-old process too? The property market is a messy, tedious business. Buying a house can take months of grueling paperwork and costly lawyer fees. In the UK, things are even worse. Your seller can accept your offer but reject it later for a higher bid, a tactic known as gazumping (though officials are finally starting to regulate it).

Most property market issues stem from a need for more trust. Complex land registries backed by reams of signed paperwork make tracking difficult, and verification requires the coordination of banks, government agencies, and lawyers. The result is an expensive, time-consuming process that many of us dread.

Blockchain, however, is trustless, removing the need for complex verification processes carried out by intermediaries. With blockchain, there is a single, transparent version of the truth, and one party can't make changes without agreement from everyone else. It's effectively tamper-proof, cutting down on paperwork and reducing fraud risk.

Perhaps most importantly, blockchain will significantly improve the medical industry. Your medical history helps doctors treat you quickly and effectively, but chances are it's fragmented across multiple healthcare providers. Incompatibilities between providers' systems slow transfer records, often requiring manual intervention. Without your complete medical history, doctors could waste money and time on tests you don't need or be unable to give you the best treatment.

Blockchain could make it easier to treat health problems by radically improving the accuracy and availability of your medical history. By creating an accessible, permanent blockchain record you own, you could instantly reveal the ailments, allergies, and lifestyle factors that help doctors diagnose and treat you. It'll also verify your identity, ensuring you're not confused with the other John Smith in the waiting room.

Finally, blockchain will give you a stronger guarantee that the goods you buy are authentic.

Currently, the bulk of supply chain management is done through EDI, a messaging system first introduced in the 1970s. Although a big step up from paper, it's far from perfect. EDI is two-way only, leaving other interested parties out of the loop. If two parties commit to defrauding a third, their activities will remain hidden (e.g., fake goods manufacturers conspiring with distributors to sell products on Amazon).

That's not the case with blockchain. Every stage of a product's journey, from its manufacture to the serial of its shipping container, is recorded and available to all stakeholders, with no possibility of cutting corners or falsifying information. It also provides an open and transparent framework that eliminates confusion and disputes.

Blockchain ensures that it's the real deal when you buy something. It's the real deal when you purchase something.

Why Is Blockchain Becoming So Popular?

Undoubtedly, the science and technology behind blockchain are gaining steam and new fans worldwide in many companies, industries, and walks of life. Why? What is it that is driving this popularity?

Blockchain technology is becoming a big deal because it's associated with cryptocurrencies and tokenized solutions.

Tokenization is splitting up units of value into ever smaller units so that more people can buy smaller units than would otherwise be possible.

This takes the existing Internet of information and communication and adds on the Internet of money and value transactions.

And the permutations that this can take are vast and varied, ranging from Bitcoin and other cryptocurrencies to Facebook's plans for an international payment system, banking, and finance, creating blockchain-based designs for faster and more secure international settlements, to real estate and other securities-based investments that allow for smaller investment into securities that used to have a high dollar value entry point, to autonomous invoicing and payments by IOT (Internet of Things) based sensors, to simply tipping online, in small amounts.

Blockchain takes the Internet - and adds money.

Money that is not controlled, regulated, or constrained by the existing national and international banking systems for fiat currencies.

And blockchain is just barely getting started. As with the Internet, as the technology matures and more easy-to-use consumer solutions appear - the more rapidly the new technology will be adopted and used.

NFTs

An NFT is, in essence, a collectible digital asset that holds value as a form of cryptocurrency and art or culture. Much like art is seen as a value-holding investment, so are NFTs. But how?

First, let's break down the term. NFT stands for a non-fungible token – a digital token that's a type of cryptocurrency, much like Bitcoin or Ethereum. But unlike a standard coin in the Bitcoin blockchain, an NFT is unique and can't be exchanged like-for-like (hence, non-fungible).

So what makes an NFT more special than a run-of-the-mill crypto coin? The file stores extra information, elevating it above pure currency and bringing it into the realm of anything. The types of NFTs are super-varied, but they could take the form of a piece of digital art or a music file – anything unique that could be stored digitally and be thought of to hold value. Essentially, they are like any other physical collector's item, but instead of receiving an oil painting on canvas to hang on your wall, for example, you get a JPG file.

NFTs are part of the Ethereum blockchain and are individual tokens with extra information. That additional information is crucial, allowing them to take the form of art, music, and video in JPG, MP3s, videos, GIFs, and more. Because they hold value, they can be bought and sold just like other types of art – and, like with physical skill; the value is set mainly by the market and demand.

However, that's not to say that only one digital version of an NFT art is available on the marketplace. In much the same way as art prints of an original are made, used, bought, and sold, copies of an NFT are still valid parts of the blockchain – but they will not hold the same value as the original.

And don't go thinking you've hacked the system by right-clicking and saving the image of an NFT, either. That won't make you a millionaire because your downloaded file won't hold the information that makes it part of the Ethereum blockchain. Make sense?

NFTs can be bought on a variety of platforms, and which you choose will depend on what it is you want to buy (for example, if you want to buy baseball cards, you're best heading to a site specifically made to sell and auction them, but other marketplaces sell more generalized pieces). You'll need a wallet specific to the platform you're buying on, and you'll need to fill that wallet with cryptocurrency.

Because of the high demand for many NFTs, they are often released as 'drops' (much like in events, when batches of tickets are often released at different times). This means a frenzied rush of eager buyers when the drop starts, so you must be registered and have your wallet topped up.

NFTs are having a moment with creators of NFT art, including artists, gamers, and brands across the spectrum of culture. Every day brings a new player to the NFT marketplace.

For artists, stepping into the NFT space adds another space and format to create and share art – and offers their admirers another way to support their work. With pieces ranging from small, quick-to-make GIFs (Rainbow Cat, above, was sold by NyanCat for $690,000) to more ambitious works, artists can offer the public a range of ways to buy art and make money.

We've talked about those making NFTs to include in video games, something that's shaking up the concept of buying assets in-game. Until now, any digital assets purchased inside a match still belonged to the game company – with gamers just buying them temporarily to use when playing the game. But NFTs mean that the ownership of assets has shifted to the actual buyer, meaning they can be bought and sold across the gaming platform with extra value based on who owns them. Games are beginning to be made that are based entirely around NFTs, proving how they are shaking up the industry.

NFTs are an attractive revenue stream for brands, as shown by all the recent brands jumping on the bandwagon. Taco Bell sold taco-themed GIFs and images (see one above) on one marketplace, and 25 sold out in just 30 minutes. Seriously. Each NFT held a $500 gift card, which the original owner could spend, which may explain their popularity initially. But these TacoCards are now selling on the secondary market, with the most expensive card selling for $3,500. And that doesn't include the gift card.

There's much money to be made in the NFT market. But you also may have heard some controversy surrounding NFTs, particularly about their impact on the climate. While NFTs are offering items in ways that are technologically advanced, the process of creating them could be more environmentally safe.

NFTs use a monster amount of energy in their creation. So much so that many protesters are worried about the genuine impact the craze could have on the environment. One piece called 'Coronavirus' consumed an incredible 192 kWh in its creation. That's equivalent to one European Union resident's total energy consumption for two weeks. But that must be a particularly huge piece, you ask? Nope, a 'simple' GIF can equate to the same consumption.

In a modern age where people are trying to be more and more green and pleasing to the planet, NFTs are providing controversy because of what they are doing to the environment.

Chapter 7: Crypto Mining

Crypto mining is a term you have heard many times if you are researching cryptocurrencies and looking to get into buying and trading. Indeed, mining is one of the most common things spoken about when people refer to crypto. It likely makes you think of an old gold miner using a pick axe to carve some gold or diamonds deep in a dark, dangerous cave.

Sure enough, mining can help you find some diamonds of your own in the form of Bitcoin. It can indeed put many cryptocurrencies in your pocket. And like the miners from the Gold Rush of the 1800s, mining can also have you walking away with nothing at all. There is indeed great reward related to mining. There is also significant risk.

So what is it? Just what is this mining thing that so many people are drawn to? Even among seasoned cryptocurrency fans, mining is a confusing sticking point that raises more questions than answers. People who have long studied crypto still do not attempt to get into mining because it is daunting and challenging. What makes it so hard? Also, is it worth it? Is it more hard work than it is worth, or is it a legitimate way to make extra money?

Crypto mining is complicated. Not only is the actual process itself complex, but so is the explanation of it. We will try to break it down as quickly and plainly as possible but do not be alarmed if it doesn't make sense.

Crypto mining is a slow, painstaking process that checks on the latest crypto transactions to verify them and ensure they are legitimate. The goal of mining is to avoid the dreaded idea of double-spending. Double spending is something that explicitly affects cryptocurrencies. It is when someone spends the same money in two places at once.

Double-spending isn't possible with physical money. If you walk into a store and spend $10 on a sandwich, you hand over the $10 bill to the employee, and it is no longer yours, and you cannot then spend it elsewhere. The same is true if you pay with a debit or credit card. Whichever financial institution you are a part of will immediately deduct the exact amount from your checking or credit card account, and that money is no longer yours to spend.

But when you pay with crypto, you can spend the money in two places simultaneously. You are paying with codes and specific keys made for each transaction. And you are doing all this without the regular checks and balances established by banks and other stable monetary systems. Cheating is possible if no one is looking.

That is where crypto mining comes into play. Mining is those checks and balances you need to ensure no one is being scammed. However, mining isn't done by an employee at your bank or an anonymous computer following a built-in procedure. Instead, mining is done by the very same people who invest in and trade crypto in the first place.

What is Mining?

Cryptocurrency mining is a process that validates Bitcoin transactions by adding them to the ledger or record of the currency, known as a blockchain. This is a challenging process. It is also a long process. Mining is not something you can casually pick up or run off of just any computer.

Miners use specialty hardware to complete the complex calculations confirming Bitcoin transactions. In simple terms, miners are trying to assemble a massive and ultra-hard puzzle. Thousands of miners are working simultaneously, trying to crack a code sent to them. They are anonymous auditors, all working towards the same goal. And whoever gets it first receives a prize: Bitcoins.

Mining continues the blockchain we spoke of before. Mining is taking important information, like all the Bitcoin transactions within the last 10 minutes, and verifying them. From there, a computer, known as the miner, must figure out a computational puzzle.

Once that miner encrypts that chunk of information or block, they can share it across the internet with other miners. Once it is verified, it is added to the existing chain. As for the computer and the user who solved the puzzle, they are rewarded with their very own Bitcoins.

Mining continues the blockchain we spoke of before. Mining is taking important information, like all the Bitcoin transactions within the last 10 minutes, and verifying them. From there, a computer, known as the miner, must figure out a computational puzzle.

Once that miner encrypts that chunk of information or block, they can share it across the internet with other miners. Once it is verified, it is added to the existing chain. As for the computer and the user who solved the puzzle, they are rewarded with their very own Bitcoins.

Can I Be A Miner?

Let's say that you have decided that you are going to take a chance and spend the time and money to build your very own cryptocurrency mining computer. You have researched the information and determined you could make a beautiful penny if your computer works.

It sure is much work, but it can and will pay off if done correctly. You stand to earn a huge profit if you have a mining rig at home, digging away at code and unlocking and encrypting blockchain. But this isn't like buying a regular computer. You cannot walk into any retail or computer store and tell them you want to buy a mining rig. No, this takes a lot more work, and you need to know what you are doing to earn your Bitcoin reward.

It is time to determine what it takes to buy and build your mining computer. If you follow these steps, have patience, and do not expect immediate success overnight, great profit might await you.

But before we get into what you need and the steps you must take, you must be reminded again that you *could* make much money by crypto mining, but it is still being determined. You may not ever make a dime off of mining. Do not walk into the crypto mining world expecting a cash windfall. Not now, maybe not ever. If it pays out, it pays out well. But there is no promise that it will ever pay out.

Types of Rigs

What is a cryptocurrency mining rig? It is a computer. But it is not a computer like the one you have at home. No, a mining rig is a computer with many graphic cards but lacks a monitor. The computer case has GPU cards, a motherboard, a cooling system, and more.

And how does it work? The rig is hooked up to the internet, of course, and the blockchain network that it needs. The blockchain network works on its own 24 hours a day and is powered by the graphic cards in the computers connected to the network.

Mining rigs often work on their own once they get up and running. They take up more space than a standard computer because of some of the protruding items included in them, so people often place mining rigs in garages or places that only stick out a little. While you *can* hook a monitor up to a mining rig and use it as a regular computer at times, most people only use them to mine. Remember, mining can be full-time, and one can work 24 hours a day.

What are the types of mining rigs you can make? There are three vastly different choices when you are building your rig.

ASIC

First up is the ASIC rig. ASIC stands for Application-Specific Integrated Circuits. These are specially-made devices created with one sole purpose in mind. This is the most important, powerful choice when you want to start a career in crypto mining. They are more than just computers, which is essential to remember. An ASIC rig is a tool made for one thing and one thing only. In this case, that one thing is mining. This is a dedicated piece of machinery built to get the job done.

Creating or buying an ASIC is hard because they are so good at what they do. Their impressive performance skills mean that many people looking to get into mining want an ASIC. That means they are hard to come by. While eventually getting your hands on an ASIC is worth it and probably your best bet at a successful mining career, finding one will take much work. You will have to rely on third-party sellers or a very, very, *very* savvy tech friend who can make one for you. Remember, this won't resemble the personal computer you use at home to surf the web or play video games. This is an entirely different beast.

There is some controversy surrounding ASIC builds too. These compelling devices have been accused of toying and messing with other mining devices on the network, and that has caused them to be subject to a lot of disdain and finger-wagging. You need to remember that when you create or buy an ASIC, especially if you care about the well-being of other miners on the network. Still, this is the most powerful and impressive computer for mining.

GPU

The GPU approach to mining is a great way to go if you want to mine and, say, watch Netflix in your spare time or play games with your friends online. They can be more than just a mining rig, unlike an ASIC build. That makes them exceedingly popular and also relatively easy to create and maintain.

151

A GPU rig is a favorite for someone looking to build their computer. While it is still difficult and requires much computer knowledge, it isn't impossible and nearly as daunting as shopping for an ASIC.

There are two types of GPU rigs: simple and dedicated miners. You can guess what a dedicated miner is. That is a GPU computer that is made only of mine. This is the right path if you want to dive headfirst into crypto mining and want to devote much time to unlocking and encrypting the blockchain.

But what if you want to share your computer with the others in your house? What if you are an avid World of Warcraft player or use your computer for homework? Then you will want the simple miner, the second type of GPU computer. You can use this device to mine *and* do other typical things that a personal computer does. The ability to choose between these two options is an excellent incentive for people looking to try their hands at mining.

What about the downsides? There is a major one when buying or making a GPU computer. That is the price. Creating or buying one of these devices can be pretty expensive. Unlike the ASIC model, a GPU relies heavily on a graphics card. Graphic cards can get expensive, especially if you are looking for a high-end one that will get the job done.

It isn't just the graphic cards that end up impacting your wallet. Your GPU will need a lot of bells and whistles and a few add-ons to keep it running in top form. You will need cooling devices and a robust electricity system. And if your GPU hits a bump in the road and needs repairs, you will have to spend a lot of money to do that effectively.

Despite its setbacks and challenges, the GPU is a beautiful way to start your mining career and can serve multiple purposes. That makes the hefty price tag more worth it.

CPU

CPU mining is the third and, at a time, the most popular way to mine. Why is CPU mining so prevalent in the crypto community? Because it is a straightforward way to mine. It is also relatively inexpensive. But when we say it is cheap, we mean building the device itself doesn't cost as much as alternatives. Upkeep and other factors of CPU mining do cost a lot and can be a massive headache as you move further in your mining career.

When we speak of the simplicity of CPU mining, we are talking about the quick setup required. You can start crypto mining right now if you have a suitable computer. You can download an app on your CPU device using the CPU method and get to mining almost immediately. This is a very enticing and promising reason for many and why scores of people tend to start CPU mining over buying or creating a GPU or ASIC rig. CPU mining takes way less effort, and getting started doesn't take much time.

But CPU mining has its drawbacks, and they are related to pricing. While creating a CPU rig isn't very expensive (in fact, you might already have a CPU rig and not even know it), the upkeep prices are frustrating and high. For one, using a CPU rig will make your electric bills skyrocket. One of the biggest complaints about mining is the cost of electricity once you get started, and, sure enough, a CPU rig will hog up a lot of your power and strain your local grid. This isn't nearly as simple as a typical computer; you are not simply flipping a switch and turning on a monitor. The system and process a CPU rig goes through to mine are long, complicated, and lengthy. It will constantly be chugging along and sucking up much power. You will see the price on your monthly statement shoot up after some time. That alone is enough reason to scare many people away.

But the electricity bill isn't the only thing that will hurt your wallet. No, the price of cooling your system and maintaining it costs just as much as the power running your rig. These machines must be tended to often; a lot can go wrong. When something goes awry, you will step in and put down a pretty penny to fix it. Altogether, these rigs will suck a lot of money out of your bank account. It will all be worth it if you successfully mine a block and get its payout. If not, you will be spending much money with minimal reward.

These three types of rigs all have their benefits and their downsides too. The most common drawback for all three models is the price. Whether with maintenance, repairs, electricity, or something else, mining on one computer costs a lot of money. A lot can go wrong, and each mis-step-misstep will drain your funds. Maintaining one of these rigs is almost more expensive than having a small child.

Consider buying and running a mining rig like a business. It will cost much money, but so does successfully owning a company. You will need to invest significant sums and hope you are rewarded with something that pays you back at the end of the process. We have spoken of how much money you can make with mining; you could generate a fortune if you find luck in the field. If you think of mining as a hobby, it will be costly. But the hefty price tag will be more palatable if you approach mining like a career or business.

How Much Will a Mining Rig Cost?

We have spoken a lot about how expensive crypto mining is. We have made no secret that it will cost you a pretty penny and may only pay out for a short time, if ever.

But how much money are we talking about? Just how hefty is the price tag related to crypto mining? How much money will it set you back? Is it worth it?

The short answer is no; it probably isn't worth it for most people. The long answer, however, is that it could be worth it if you do it the right way and are comfortable spending a lot of cash. This isn't some hobby you pick up at your convenience; it is something you must dedicate a lot of time and energy to.

When building your computer, you will create a large chunk of change to create a rig that can do the job right. The graphic card needed for a CPU mining rig is at least $700. Some cost quite a bit more than that, too; it depends on what you are comfortable using. Remember, cutting corners and going cheap with any part of your rig will cost you in the long run and affect your computer's ability to mine successfully. It is hard to spend money like this, but it is even harder to do all this work for absolutely nothing while other computers race by you in terms of power.

The graphic card alone will hit your bank account hard. From there, the other components aren't much cheaper. There are examples of people building a crypto mining rig for around $3,000, but that is the bare minimum of what you can spend, and that sort of computer will not be very promising or deliver many chances for success.

On the other hand, some people have spent more than $10,000 on their rigs. That is more expensive than many cars. Even then, there is no guarantee of success. You can spend thousands of dollars on a rig and still walk away empty-handed. Are your chances improved based on how much money you spend? Yes, they are. But do not think spending $10,000 automatically means you will be racking in the Bitcoin.

The price of the computer isn't the only thing you will consider when getting into mining. Remember the electricity you will be using to mine. The total can add up fast and send some people straight into bankruptcy court.

We all have electricity bills and are familiar with their average price. You know that during the height of winter and summer, your power bill is going to skyrocket because of the consumption needed to keep you and your family warm or cool. But even the highest bill you've come across pales compared to what you will experience if you start crypto mining at home.

Research has shown that the cheapest electricity cost for mining a single Bitcoin is more than $3,000. That is an astronomically high number, and it's on the lower end of the spectrum. You will have to spend about $3,000 to mine a single coin in the cheapest states in the nation. If you live in a state with higher power prices, you could drop $6,000 to mine your Bitcoin. That quote, on top of the cost of creating and maintaining your rig, is tough to swallow. It is tough to accept if you aren't getting anything in return for all that cash spent. At that rate, it could take weeks or months to get a return on your investment, and that is only if your rig works perfectly and is lucky enough to mine a coin.

You can see the risk and rewards associated with crypto mining regarding how much you will spend. The cost of building and maintaining your rig is enough to scare many people away from attempting to make money this way. But when you remember the value of your rewarded Bitcoin, it sounds more promising. Just remember that, like everything related to cryptocurrency, your success isn't guaranteed, and it is doubtful that it will happen quickly.

Is Mining Legal?

Crypto mining, like cryptocurrency as a whole, isn't legal all over the globe. While most nations allow cryptos like Bitcoin and other altcoins, some countries do not allow them. Live in Egypt, Ecuador, Nepal, Pakistan, and Morocco. You will not be able to purchase or trade cryptocurrency and will not be able to mine.

However, in other countries, you can buy and mine freely. That doesn't mean it will always be that way, however. As cryptocurrency becomes more popular and disrupts the traditional monetary system, more and more people in power, like politicians, have come forward, pushing back against it and hoping to limit or outright restrict it. If that happens in the country you live in, your ability to mine and buy crypto will become a thing of the past and could put you in serious legal jeopardy.

This is one of the other risks of crypto mining. The crypto landscape is changing constantly, for better and worse. It is not only the value of coins that remains volatile. The opinion and future outlook for cryptocurrency also always feel in flux. In the months and years ahead, some nations will successfully ban crypto and the ability to buy, trade, and mine coins.

This unpredictability is a considerable drawback to mining. Imagine spending thousands upon thousands of dollars on mining. Imagine starting to make a profit off of it. Imagine it becomes banned in your region, and you are effectively breaking the law. All of that money, all of that time, all of that energy - down the drain. That is the risk you run by participating in an industry still seen as new and different and a bit suspicious by those in power.

It is important to note that if you live in a country that hasn't limited or banned cryptocurrency, you are doing nothing wrong by crypto mining. You are free to do so and should feel no shame. But you do need to consider the political and economic environment you live in. If there is a chance that cryptocurrency could be banned where you live, you should proceed with caution before you start to put time and money into becoming a crypto miner.

What About Mining Pools?

You may have read about mining pools as an intelligent and cheaper alternative to creating and running your mining rig. This is an easier route, especially if you want to save money. However, it has its drawbacks as well.

What is a mining pool? It is a group of miners all working together to unlock and encrypt a Bitcoin and earn a reward. As you can imagine, the resulting coin doesn't just go to one miner. Instead, all participants split the payout. That means the whole lump sum won't just go to you, even if your computer is the one that finally cracks the code. You are agreeing to split the earnings with those in your pool. That is terrible news if you want all the Bitcoin for yourself. But it also means you can reap a massive windfall of money even if your rig isn't the one to find success. These mining pools are run by third parties who rely on the network of computers in each collection. This is indeed a more straightforward and far more profitable way to mine. The work's weight isn't on you and your rig; it is spread evenly across your pool. However, it is again important to note that there is no sure thing in mining, even when you are part of a pool.

Bottom Line: Should I Crypto Mine?

Like everything related to cryptocurrency, there needs to be more clarity around mining. Some people feel it is a sure thing, a great way to get rich quickly. Others, however, think the payout related to mining is impossible and that all it will ever be is a massive waste of time and money.

The reality is somewhere in the middle. No, it is not a get-rich-quick scheme and should never be considered one. And it is also not a complete and utter waste of time. Likely, you will never get rich by crypto mining, but you stand a chance at making some money. Will that amount of money make the price of computing and electricity worth it? That depends on your success and what you are comfortable with.

What is a Fork?

You have heard of a fork before but probably haven't heard of one about finance, have you? But forks are a significant part of financial institutions, especially cryptocurrency. And they can make or break an entire cryptocurrency.

A hard fork is when nodes of the newest version of a blockchain no longer accept the older version(s), which creates a permanent divergence from the previous version of the blockchain.

Adding a new rule to the code essentially creates a fork in the blockchain: one path follows the new, upgraded blockchain, and the other continues along the old path. Generally, after a short time, those on the old chain will realize their blockchain version is outdated or irrelevant and quickly upgrade to the latest version.

A fork in a blockchain can occur in any crypto-technology platform—not only Bitcoin. That is because blockchains and cryptocurrencies work the same way no matter which crypto platform they're on. You may think of the blocks in blockchains as cryptographic keys that move memory. Because the miners in a blockchain set the rules that drive the memory in the network, these miners understand the new rules.

However, all miners must agree on the new rules and what comprises a valid block in the chain. So when you want to change those rules, you need to "fork it"—like a fork in a road— to indicate that there's been a change in or a diversion to the protocol. The developers can then update the software to reflect the new rules.

Through this forking process, various digital currencies with names similar to Bitcoin have come to be: bitcoin cash, bitcoin gold, and others. For the casual cryptocurrency investor, it can be difficult to tell the difference between these cryptocurrencies and to map the various forks onto a timeline. To help sort this out, we have composed a history of the essential Bitcoin hard forks of the past several years.

There are several reasons why developers may implement a hard fork, such as correcting essential security risks found in older versions of the software, adding new functionality, or reversing transactions—such as when the Ethereum blockchain created a hard fork to reverse the hack on the Decentralized Autonomous Organization.

After the hack, the Ethereum community almost unanimously voted in favor of a hard fork to roll back transactions that siphoned off tens of millions of dollars worth of digital currency by an anonymous hacker. The hard fork also helped DAO token holders get their ether funds returned.

The proposal for a hard fork did not exactly unwind the network's transaction history. Instead, it relocated the funds tied to the DAO to a newly created smart contract to let the original owners withdraw their funds.

DAO token holders could withdraw ETH at approximately 1 ETH to 100 DAO. The DAO curators withdrew and distributed the extra balance of tokens and any ether that remained due to the hard fork to provide "failsafe protection" for the organization.

Chapter 8: How To Stay Safe with Crypto

We have examined and talked about some of the many upsides of investing in Bitcoin and cryptocurrencies and the incredible power of blockchain. There are quick returns on investment, the accessibility of starting a new account, and the lack of restrictions from government bodies attempting to slow you down. Indeed, there is much to celebrate about crypto and the new and easy ways it allows to make money and become a part of such an exciting market.

There hasn't been anything like cryptocurrency, and its benefits are seemingly endless and truly impressive. It is a breath of fresh air to investors, bringing in newcomers who have never invested or traded before and want to get in on the ground floor of something special.

Unfortunately, it also brings out a fair number of scammers. As we have said before, there needs to be more clarity about cryptocurrency; a lot that people need to learn and a lot that is easy to inflate or muddle. A certain vagueness comes with cryptocurrency because the media needs to report and describe it accurately and because of its somewhat complicated nature. If you need to become more familiar with technology, cryptocurrency may make you scratch your head. However, there are still people looking to invest even though they need help understanding what they are doing. That is a recipe for disaster, and a scammer's dream come true.

Scamming has sadly become a substantial part of the cryptocurrency world because of the confusion around crypto and the lack of regulation and oversight from significant institutions. However, you are not destined to be taken advantage of by a scammer. There are ways to avoid these criminals looking to make a buck off of you. You need to be prepared and aware of what to look for because, sadly, navigating through scammers is becoming a regular part of cryptocurrency.

What Are Crypto Dangers?

The unfortunate thing about cryptocurrency scams is that there are many of them, and they seem to be only growing. Scammers have found many ways to capitalize on new investors and profit from their lack of knowledge and overall need for clarification about buying and trading crypto.

The truth is that crypto scamming has become a significant industry, and many people make far more money ripping off others than actually investing in crypto itself. In 2019, more than $4 billion was made by scammers. More than many companies make $4 billion is an astonishing amount of money. You can see why so many nefarious people worldwide want to get in on such a scandalous way of making money.

Scams are a scary thing. Not only are they scary because they can steal your money, your information, and, ultimately, your safety. They are also tricky because they hurt the overall health of Bitcoin and cryptocurrency. When a scam becomes prominent and well-known, it scares people away from investing in Bitcoin. As we have noted before, the strength of the crypto market relies on peoples' faith and trust in the system. If that waivers, the entire market will decline and trend downward. So while any scam is terrible for those affected, it can cause a ripple effect that will only harm the future of Bitcoin and the investments of those involved.

Many scams exist and are running rampant across the web. The most common scams would be fake Bitcoin exchanges online or Ponzi schemes. Let's start with the Ponzi scheme first since it is something you have seen in all sorts of industries and have for decades.

The Ponzi Scheme

A Ponzi scheme is when you pay into some business or investment with a promise of a significant return on your investment. It may be a small business that needs some starting cash but will pay you back your money with interest in less than a year. Maybe a brokerage investor is starting his firm and looking to put your money into some sure-thing stocks that will make you a massive profit in no time. Whatever the situation, a Ponzi scheme needs your money upfront with the guarantee that you will get it back - and then some - shortly after that.

The tricky thing about Ponzi schemes is that investors often see some money, which usually ensures that everything is above the board and properly working. In reality, though, the schemer is paying out profits to early investors using the latest batch of money. As long as more people are putting into the pot, the scammer can continue to distribute just a little bit of money to those who have invested and lure them into paying more. In reality, there isn't nearly as much money to go around as they promise, and eventually, the house of cards will collapse, and the significant sums promised will suddenly vanish.

The most unfortunate thing about Ponzi schemes is that it is tough for scammed investors to get their money back. They can never get back the total amount they put in because the scammer has often spent it all on him or herself. That is true for Bitcoin scams too.

How does a Bitcoin Ponzi scheme work? Usually, they promise to make the entire idea of Bitcoin trading and investing easy on you. They say they will remove the middleman by buying crypto and do all the hard work for you. All you need to do is provide payment, and they will invest for you but will still show you the progress your coins are making and will keep you up to date on how successful your investment is.

The problem is that they likely need to invest more. These scams hope they can trick you by showing you fake statements with falsified numbers. You will think you are doing great and will not ask to sell your coins. Or you may ask for just a sliver of your profits so far, which they can afford to part with. However, they are giving you other peoples' money while taking in even more to keep their scam alive. The moment the system is figured out, it will collapse, and no one will walk away with anything.

Another Ponzi approach to Bitcoin revolves around crypto mining. There have been several instances of up-and-coming businesses offering you to invest in mining. As we have discussed, crypto mining is a highly complicated process requiring much work and processing power to create, encrypt, and verify the ever-growing blockchain. However, if your system is one of the lucky ones to mine a block successfully, you will be rewarded with a Bitcoin, which can net you thousands of dollars.

Schemers across the globe know that mining is a very confusing thing that most people know little about. But they also know that many people know the great payout possible if you are successful in mining. So these schemers lure people in with the promise of a significant sum of cash at the end. They promise they have the computing power and the know-how; they only need the money to get things up and running.

In 2019, a band of scammers was busted after creating a business called BitClub Network. They ran the scam for years. They solicited more than $722 million from investors by promising them a part in a giant crypto mining pool. They swore up and down that significant profits were coming and that investors could make even more money if they recruited others to join in. In the end, the investors walked away empty-handed. The Ponzi scheme is an easy trap to fall into. It plays upon your desire to make money quickly and without much effort. Scammers know precisely what to say and how to lure you in. They are smooth talkers who make themselves seem knowledgeable, friendly, and eager to help. In reality, they are preying upon those who do not know better. It is a horrible way to make money and one you should always look out for.

Make sure you see proof of your profits and do not invest in shady businesses that cannot prove how much you are making. Fact-check any potential scam, look into and do some research online. Ideally, avoiding any situation that could be a Ponzi scheme is best. Get-rich-quick plans seem too good to be true because they almost always are. You will make money slower and more efficiently than some say, so if someone tells you you can, you should be very weary.

Fake Bitcoin Exchanges

South Korea, 2017. Financial authorities made a significant bust in that country. The alleged criminals were running a scam called BitKRX. What did BitKRX do? They promised investors that they were the country's most powerful Bitcoin trading platform and took millions upon millions of dollars from people looking to turn a profit and make money off cryptocurrency.

These sorts of fake websites are becoming all too popular over the years. The bigger Bitcoin becomes, the more significant these scams become too. They prey upon folks who do not know much about investing and do not know the intricate details of buying and trading Bitcoin. They know they want to make money at the end of the day, and these fake exchange sites promise that. But they are also reasonable rates that are unheard of and frankly unreasonable. They promise you will invest for next to nothing, and the process will be painless and quick. In reality, they are taking advantage of you and simply stealing your money. None of it is buying Bitcoin or other altcoins; none of it is going into any market. They are merely pocketing your cash, and you are left with nothing.

Fake Bitcoin Exchanges are tough to combat because it is so easy for scammers to create authentic-looking sites that feel like the real thing. And for those who have yet to do the proper research, they are easy to fall for. Many people assume there are many real cryptocurrency exchange sites across the web. In reality, there are far less than you think. The moment you hear of a brand new exchange site promising too-good-to-be-true rates, you need to proceed with extreme caution because it is likely a scam and a way for you to lose it all and gain nothing.

The truth is that investing in Bitcoin should be done through one of the few genuinely reputable online exchanges. They are easy to find; a short Google search can find the most popular and reliable ones. Anything aside from those few is not worth your time. Refrain from trying to make extra money when finding an exchange, and be aware of finding the next best thing full of unheard-of rates and promises. You should take This part of Bitcoin trading seriously and avoid all risks. If you make much money off Bitcoin, it will not be because of the exchange site you buy into. Instead, you will make money by investing wisely and trading at the right time. Do not fall for a scammer who will tell you otherwise.

Scamming Emails and Fake Sites

Scamming emails have grown in popularity over the last few decades, and you cannot go a few days with some junk email promising you something rewarding and out of this world. These emails immediately go into your junk folder, and with good reason: they are trash. But that doesn't stop them from coming.

Why do spam emails still exist decades after the creation of modern email? Because someone is falling for it. It may be hard to believe, but these scammers make their money somehow. Even though nine out of ten people can recognize and ignore a scam email, one person may go for it. That is sometimes all a scammer needs to make their money.

The same is valid for spamming emails related to Bitcoin investing. Most people will not fall for it. Most people will recognize spam as spam, immediately ignore it, and keep it from wasting time. But there are people out there who need to become more experienced with Bitcoin and will be tricked into responding to a spam email, and then they will soon be losing their money.

They are creating an email address and official-looking correspondence that feels like the real thing isn't hard. There are many ways to impress potential investors and dupe them into giving away money. A spam email creates a letterhead and logo that looks real. These scam artists will state that they work for an effective and reputable service. They will use that company's artwork and logo in their emails. They will also create email addresses that look just like the real thing. But upon closer inspection, it would become evident that they are using old tricks that scammers have had for ages. They will replace the letter O with a zero or something along those lines, something that will trick the reader into thinking that things are valid and legitimate.

All the scams associated with Bitcoin and cryptocurrency exploit people looking to get rich quickly. That is an easy way for them to get their foot in the door and promise something that everyone wants: money, lots of it. The desire to get rich quickly is one you will need to disregard when you start investing in cryptocurrencies altogether. Do not expect to make millions overnight. Instead, you should be prepared to make your money slowly but steadily if you make the right choices and invest and trade smartly. You look in the wrong place if you attempt to make tons of money quickly.

There are other ways that scammers can take money from you. There are fake mobile apps that aren't legitimate and will only drain you of cash; malware is embodied on scammer sites that will hack into your account and take your banking or email information. There are even other scams related to Bitcoin like people claiming to be from the IRS and demanding you pay back taxes on sums you raised via cryptocurrencies. If you are not paying attention, there are plenty of ways for people to make money from you. What we listed are just some of the many approaches scammers will take. You must pay attention, stay informed and always keep yourself safe. Investing in Bitcoin offers you the chance to make money; that is true. But falling victim to a Bitcoin scam only promises heartbreak and financial ruin.

Will Crypto Be Banned? Why Do People Distrust It?

As you have heard repeatedly, there is a level of distrust aimed at Bitcoin and cryptocurrency that is unparalleled. Many people do not understand Bitcoin and believe in the most hyped and sensationalized conspiracies. Some people believe that Bitcoin is only used by hackers, scammers, and people who want to steal your hard-earned cash. Other people think that Bitcoin can easily *be* hacked and stolen, and there is no reason to invest because it will be taken from you by some criminal computer pro. Other people think that it cannot be used anywhere or that it has no value at all.

Many confused and unfounded thoughts about Bitcoin have led to rampant speculation and skewed biases and views. However, others know better. Some people know the particulars of Bitcoin and cryptocurrency and how it works. They are realists; they understand the benefits and the disadvantages of Bitcoin. Still, they choose to rail against Bitcoin and fight tooth and nail to ensure it doesn't find a solid footing in the modern world. Why do these people fight so vigorously against Bitcoin and its potential? What are they afraid of? Why do they hate it so much?

Why is such anger directed at Bitcoin by the people who should know much better?

(Traditional) Money is Power

It is important to remember just how powerful and essential money is. There is no way to deny that, nothing to debate about that statement. People say that money is the root of all evil, and that may be true. But it is also the root of all power. And when someone has power, they want to hold onto it.

It is worth noting that someone isn't evil just because they want to control their power and keep things as they are. There is a solid argument to be made there. The world's entire course can collapse when things change too drastically or quickly. Some people legitimately want to hold onto their gained power because they genuinely believe the alternative could spell doom for economies and the people within them. Not everyone who wants to keep the status quo strong is a money-hungry monster. People have goals, expectations, biases, and desires. It isn't wrong to fight for what you genuinely believe is right.

Many people who have gained much power in governments and major corporations have done so with money. They have made much money and spent much money to get to where they are now. They have done this using fiat currencies. Fiat is a term used to describe conventional currencies, like the Dollar, Yen, etc.

The thing about fiat currencies is that they only really have value because the governments say they do. For example, the United States government has said that the dollar is the only valuable currency in the United States. If they came out one day and declared that seashells were the new, only accepted currency in America, seashells would now have value, and the dollar would be a flimsy piece of paper that meant nothing. Any tangible assets do not technically back fiat currencies. There is a term that you may see when reading about money. It says "backed by the full faith and credit" of the government. That means the government believes in that currency, which is why it is valuable. It has been chosen, deemed appropriate, and that is why you use it.

As technology has advanced, that means less and less to some people. But for those in power, the fiat currency that nations have used for generations must stay the only, unrivaled form of payment. That is the sort of currency they have amassed that is the sort of currency that makes the world go around, that is the sort of currency that keeps corporations thriving and the stock market booming. If fiat currencies didn't have as much value because they had legitimate competition, the power wouldn't be as strong. Money is power, and only one type of money can be recognized: the money that the powerful use. That is fiat currency.

Governments want to avoid new forms of currency because they need to learn how to handle it. They must learn how to monitor, tax, or control it properly. Current governments have great control over how much money is in circulation and how much it gets taxed. They can track money because they handle money. If fiat currencies lost their power and more people turned to cryptocurrency, the government would not be as in control, and that is something they desperately want to avoid.

Without control over currency, governments of the world would not be able to control fiscal policy, crime, and the world of business. Remember, the financial elite who control the puppet politicians have a lot invested in the current system and will do everything they can to keep it in place. They will even create their own Central Bank Digital Currency (CPDC) to continue to control the system. But that will only help Bitcoin to thrive and not shut it down.

Those in power think the concept behind Bitcoin or cryptocurrency is good. Some think the idea is revolutionary and essential; some genuinely believe in branching off and starting something new. However, many people know that things can get messy if the power is divided between those who currently have it and others. What will happen to the economy? What will happen to the business industry? So many things would be altered if cryptocurrency became more mainstream. Most notably, the balance of power would shift. They do not want that.

Unfortunately, that is why so many have turned to innuendo and downright conspiracies and lies about cryptocurrency. Some politicians and industrialists have come out and said that they do not want to see cryptocurrency thrive because it stands a chance of disrupting how things are currently run. That is an honest view of things. Others have spread misinformation about Bitcoin and all forms of cryptocurrency, saying it is easily hacked, has no value, and will drain your bank account and leave you in ruins.

The truth is that many of these people know the reality: that cryptocurrency isn't easily hackable but, in fact, very safe. Bitcoin does have value, just not based on the dollar or fiat currency. Lastly, it will not drain your bank account and will not leave you in ruins. It is less dangerous and more safe than the dollar and many other forms of traditional money.

But the problem doesn't just lie in the fact that some people do not like cryptocurrencies and Bitcoin. There is no crime there. Nothing can stop them from hating Bitcoin and spreading falsehoods about it. The problem arises when these same people hold government office, use their power to spread lies further, and push laws that limit people's ability to use and buy Bitcoin openly. That is when things cross over into the downright wrong.

While some genuinely want what is best for consumers and buyers, others do not wish for Bitcoin to become popular because that means they stand a chance of losing the vast amount of power they have gathered over the years. Often, you see these people spreading rumors or misinformation about Bitcoin in hopes that it will prevent the cryptocurrency from finding a new home with investors all over the globe.

These people, along with those who do not trust the power of Bitcoin and are coming from a place of genuine care and concern, sometimes come together to pressure lawmakers to pass legislation that will stop Bitcoin in its tracks. So far, no one has been able to stop the development of Bitcoin in the most significant countries, like the United States. In this country and others, Bitcoins remain free and unregulated. But that hasn't stopped attempts to limit or outright ban it.

States Fight For (And Against) Bitcoin

Bitcoin was initially seen as a stateless - and nationless - digital currency that could be accepted everywhere and would have no regulations no matter where you were spending it. One of the most exciting aspects of the premise behind Bitcoin was that you could use it anywhere and use it on anything. There should be no reason why Bitcoin shouldn't be universally legal and unchecked in all jurisdictions, not just in the United States but worldwide.

However, that has yet to be the case. As stated, many countries worldwide have enacted specific rules for and against Bitcoin and other cryptocurrencies. The same is valid for individual countries in the United States. Since the federal government has so far tried to stay out of the cryptocurrency battle, deciding not to regulate it and let the people run it themselves, some states have stepped up to either support or push back against the rise in popularity of Bitcoin.

Some states are better than others for Bitcoin. Because of state-level laws signed by numerous governors, Bitcoin is more efficiently used and traded, bought in some states, and more complex to come by and support in others.

For example, New York has long been a nemesis of Bitcoin. Considering how many people of power associated with Wall Street live in New York state, this isn't surprising. It would stand to reason that these influential people would use their connections with the governor to limit the power of Bitcoin. That is precisely what happened because New York has never supported Bitcoin. All online exchanges must disclose their global client base to state officials in New York. To some, that sounds like a massive invasion of privacy. This is just an example of the ways that New York State has tried to stymie the power of Bitcoin.

New York Governor Andrew Cuomo created a Bitcoin task force to study the use and intricacies of Bitcoin, so there may be changes in the future if the task force finds nothing to fear with Bitcoin. Supporters of cryptocurrency are hoping that's the case. Another state that has come out swinging against cryptocurrency and Bitcoin is Rhode Island. Their senator, Sheldon Whitehouse, has long railed against Bitcoin and has said it is a way for foreign interference in America's business. He was a significant supporter of state-wide legislation that heavily taxed online exchanges and all cryptocurrency transactions. This shows that not only Sheldon Whitehouse thinks that Bitcoin and crypto can be a tool for foreign governments and adversaries.

Other states, such as Arizona, have created specific laws and taxes that oppose welcoming Bitcoin. This has hurt the base of supporters in those states and has made significant pushback from cryptocurrency fans. It flies in the face of the ideas and purpose behind Bitcoin, which has always been about a universal currency that governments would not hold back because it didn't need them. Bitcoin can thrive independently without any federal body of power's regulation, oversight, or help.

But it cannot exist without them. The fact is that Bitcoin would always go head-to-head with governments. There is no way around that. These strict laws being pushed by certain nations and states show that Bitcoin may exist outside the system but remains inside it significantly.

Thankfully, not all states are trying to limit the power and strength of Bitcoin. Other regions in America are supportive of cryptocurrency. For example, Colorado passed a law 2018 encouraging state agencies to use blockchain technology to keep their confidential records secret. That was seen as a massive sign of support for the crypto community. This was also matched by legislation allowing cryptocurrency donations in political campaigns and a bill that exempted cryptocurrencies from specific securities regulations. Colorado has proven that it isn't afraid of Bitcoin. It sees the value in the technology behind it.

Although it is usually known for its conservative politics that many would think could put them on the opposing side of Bitcoin and cryptocurrency, the state of Texas has shown itself to be an ally in advancing Bitcoin-related technology. That state has become a hub of crypto mining facilities; multiple central crypto mining locations exist throughout Lone Star State. This is partly due to the cheap cost of electricity and energy in Texas since using power is a significant part of crypto-mining, and the more expensive it is, the more complex the mining becomes.

But Texas has welcomed many mining companies because of the business, income, and employment it brings.

California, unsurprisingly, is another state which has tried to embrace Bitcoin and cryptocurrency. Their governor signed a law 2014 that affirmed that "various forms of alternative currency such as digital currency" are legal payments when purchasing goods. Many major crypto companies in the world are located in California, such as Kraken, Ripple, Coinbase, and more.

The most crypto-friendly state in the union would be Wyoming. The least populated state is among the most engaging and positive regarding Bitcoin and cryptocurrencies. Wyoming has passed multiple laws to recognize and support cryptocurrencies. Their state legislature even created a bill that grants digital currencies the same legal status as other money. Because of their extended support for cryptocurrencies, including Bitcoin, Wyoming has become home to many crypto companies and has received its fair share of praise from the community that uses them. Wyoming might not be the first place you think of when you talk crypto, but it should be. It has shown time and again that it supports the future of cryptocurrency.

Some states favor Bitcoin and will do much to help advance it; others are against it and pushing legislation limiting it. The fight continues and will for some time. As long as the federal government stays out of the fray, it will be up to individual states to decide how Bitcoin and cryptocurrencies are regulated. Though that may mean it is sometimes a tough road, crypto fans support this approach because many need more confidence in federal officials. They fear that crypto proves too much of a risk and danger to the federal government, so they prefer they stay out of the arguments altogether. The more hands-off the government is, the better.

However, that doesn't mean the United States government has never dipped its toes in the fight and limited cryptocurrency. They have created an outright ban on at least one cryptocurrency. That decision spotlighted how politics and foreign affairs can mix and potentially make a massive mess for the future of cryptocurrency.

Chapter 9: What's Next For Crypto and Blockchain

What Could Happen With Crypto in the Future?

Cryptocurrency and blockchain have become incredible global phenomena in just a short time. No one can argue that it could become even more powerful and thriving in the years ahead. However, some people say about what a future for crypto looks like. Which direction will it go?

Many people see Bitcoin as the currency of the future, so speculation about what is next for it has run rampant since its inception.

So, what does Bitcoin's future hold? Many people think it is on the verge of a significant breakthrough that will take it further than ever. What would that breakthrough look like? Some speculate that a major retailer will begin accepting Bitcoin shortly. If a business such as Target, Walmart, or Amazon started to take Bitcoin as a currency, that would be a game changer. If that were to happen, you can expect to see the value of Bitcoin skyrocket by leaps and bounds in no time at all.

If a significant retailer welcomed Bitcoin, it would send a strong message to other businesses worldwide that cryptocurrency is here to stay and can be trusted and accepted safely. It would also send a massive message to average investors across the globe that significant business icons are now warming to the idea of cryptocurrency. That would drive people to online exchanges, looking to spend their money on crypto finally, and that would only make the industry boom even more.

If a retailer started accepting Bitcoin shortly, an immediate ripple effect would be felt and seen. It would increase the value of all cryptocurrencies, not just Bitcoin. People would be looking to make money off crypto and wouldn't want to focus solely on Bitcoin. However, Bitcoin itself would become even more significant and even more wanted. Headlines and news stories would splash across every newspaper and network on Earth. It would be one of the biggest business stories of the year. This possible development is what many people have been waiting for. Fans of Bitcoin have been anticipating the day that a more significant retail business takes the first step and starts taking Bitcoin as payment at their locations. For years now, the holy grail has been Amazon since Bitcoin users know how convenient spending Bitcoin at Amazon could be. However, that online market hasn't embraced the idea yet, and Amazon has refused to budge on its resistance to Bitcoin.

Bitcoin proponents have been focusing on other retailers in hopes that they take the first step since Amazon has seemed hesitant over the years. They have their sights set on places like Best Buy and other businesses that provide many customers with the latest technology, gear, and devices. Some campaigns have convinced these businesses to accept Bitcoin and cryptocurrencies, but more headway has yet to be made. The possibility of this happening remains the biggest question for the future of cryptocurrencies. This is the most significant step for it to become mainstream, which many crypto fans see as necessary.

If a significant retailer remains outside the reach of Bitcoin shortly, that isn't the end of the road for crypto. No matter what, the future for crypto remains bright. Why? Because more people are flocking to crypto than ever before. Year after year, the currency attracts new investors looking to enter the market, and every time someone buys in, the value only goes up. That is why you have seen the price of various cryptocurrencies, most especially Bitcoin, skyrocket over the years.

However, if Bitcoin and other crypto fail to have some large name companies latch onto them and join in, you can expect to see their need to be clarified and met with trepidation from casual investors. You can also expect many successful business people and politicians to continue to rail against crypto and attempt to bring it down.

In the years ahead, a more significant fight will likely be waged against Bitcoin and its peers. We have already seen that beginning in India, Egypt, and the United States. Cryptocurrencies have made billions of dollars quickly, and money equals power in most countries. And new energy can be scary for those who have held old power for a long time. It is seen as a new threat that can unseat those in control and needs to be kept in check before it becomes too strong. Many Fortune 500 CEOs are looking to reel crypto in the years ahead, and they have mighty friends who can make that happen.

As for blockchain, the future potential is endless. As more and more major companies and industries discover the power of blockchain, it will only grow in popularity and continue to become more impactful worldwide. Blockchain started solely to facilitate the use of Bitcoin and cryptocurrencies. But it has become part of the healthcare industry, shipping and transportation, automobile companies, and even payroll technology.

Blockchain has never had such a promising future. It has become more than just a companion technology for Bitcoin and cryptocurrency. It has taken on a life of its own and still stands a chance to alter nearly every business in the world - if they are willing to accept it.

Chapter 10: How Blockchain Will Affect Your Life, Your Friend's Life & Your Families Lives!

What are the Real World Applications of Blockchain

Blockchain is already spreading worldwide and significantly affecting everything it touches in only the best of ways. What are some of the industries that are benefitting the most from blockchain and all it provides?

Healthcare

Take the pharmaceutical industry, for example. New rules to ensure drug integrity from manufacturing to consumption could save up to a million lives each year. Life sciences and healthcare companies create unique serial numbers for units of medication and pieces of equipment, which are scanned, captured, and verified at their point of origin.

Applied correctly, blockchain can take track-and-trace serialization to the next level, cutting costs, elevating security and trust, eliminating error-prone data movements, and enabling real-time supply chain transparency. Additional verified information is appended using blockchain as each item moves through the supply chain. These data blocks cannot be tampered with and are collectively validated by all stakeholders. The result is an end-to-end system that is simpler and more secure than anything we have seen before. It is more private, transparent, and efficient, with less risk, and meets and exceeds global serialization requirements.

The world of fashion is also embracing blockchain. CGS, an organization providing business applications, enterprise learning systems, and outsourcing services, is hearing from fashion, apparel, and consumer goods clients that they are looking at new ways to streamline the supply chain through blockchain.

Food Safety

From the supply chain perspective, blockchain can enable trust between trading partners and consumers. With blockchain technology, consumers can see the garment's entire lifecycle from the farm to the shelf. Consumers are going from blind trust to a complete understanding of the journey of that garment. With blockchain, an item's sustainability and compliance can be tracked on the raw materials and manufacturing processes."

Food safety is a significant industry that is incredibly important. Without it, all of society would suffer. And now, blockchain is arriving to make the entire system run better, smoother, and more efficiently.

IBM is partnering with food suppliers, including Dole, Nestlé, and Walmart, to regulate food safety better using blockchain. In the global food supply chain industry, all growers, suppliers, processors, distributors, retailers, regulators, and consumers can gain permission access to information about the origin and state of food in their transactions. All members of the ecosystem can use the blockchain network to trace contaminated foods to their source in a short amount of time to ensure they are quickly removed from store shelves.

The World Wildlife Fund is also using blockchain to better track seafood if you can believe it.

Consumers are calling for fully-traceable seafood that does not come from illegal fisheries or those that abuse human rights. Wholesale and retail seafood buyers are asking for improvements in transparency and traceability to reduce the risk of their brands being associated with dubious and illegal activities. Layered into the real-time information coming from other electronic technology platforms, blockchains can provide the unprecedented supply chain transparency and traceability that retailers and consumers want.

Oil & Gas

Oil and gas companies have taken to blockchain too, and they're already making millions more because of it. Blockchain in the energy sector allows users to monitor transactions, control output, and verify the origin of certificates.

There is a blockchain-based trading project with participants such as BP, Shell, Statoil, Gunvor, Koch Supply & Trading, and Mercuria commercial enterprises and, from banking, ABN Amro, ING, and Societe Generale. They developed a digital platform for managing transactions in the energy market. The project's authors aim to reduce the dependence on traditional paper contracts and the kilograms of paper documentation used in favor of a digital registry.

Blockchain will allow the energy sector to reduce operating costs, accelerate domestic trading operations for all its energy supply chains and increase the reliability of their operations. Most projects are currently under development, but industry representatives have long understood their relevance and importance. Undoubtedly, over time, the number of blockchain solutions in various sectors of the economy will increase significantly, and the benefits of their implementation will become quite apparent.

Automotive

Blockchain in the automotive industry is seen as a tool for storing and transmitting data by smart cars. In addition, the technology can be used to store data about specific cars in various registries. Blockchain will not allow for the falsification of data about a car. For example, after a vehicle is put on the market, all data about it, including information about service and repairs, will be stored using blockchain. As a result, the owner of a car will be able, at any time, to check the number of repairs it has undergone, accident data, and other information.

Auto industry players have been exploring the possibilities of blockchain for several years. Two years ago, Toyota announced a new program to introduce blockchain into its innovative car technology, where a distributed registry is used as the basis for exchanging data between intelligent vehicles. A similar project is being implemented by General Motors, which patented its technology in 2019. Volkswagen is developing blockchain technology that allows intelligent cars to exchange information about road conditions. According to its developers, the project could reduce the number of accidents caused by poor-quality road surfaces, challenging weather conditions, or other accidents.

Election Fraud

It's not only financial transactions that work with blockchain but any data transmission. This system infrastructure benefits voting because voting is a small piece of high-value data. Out of necessity, modern voting systems are primarily stuck in the last century, and those that want to vote must leave their homes and submit paper ballots to a local authority. Why not bring this process online? Some have tried, but it has proven difficult to put faith in the results due to significant security gaps.

Blockchain can solve the many problems discovered in these early attempts at online voting. A blockchain-based voting application does not concern itself with the security of its Internet connection because any hacker with access to the terminal cannot affect other nodes. Voters can effectively submit their votes without revealing their identity or political preferences to the public. Officials can count votes with absolute certainty, knowing that each ID can be attributed to one vote, no fakes can be created, and that tampering is impossible.

Voter apathy has seen the number of people showing up to cast their votes dwindle in recent years, even as it has become more critical. In America alone, the number of people who vote is far lower than those who *can*. Apathy in the voting booth hurts the country in many ways. With an involved populace, the government can go down the right path. People need to be engaged, and people need to care. Blockchain can help people believe in voting much more than now.

These miserable and sad numbers would rise by providing an irrefutable and easy way to vote from one's phone or PC. Blockchain is paving the way for a direct democracy, where people can decide the course of policy themselves rather than rely on representatives to do it for them. While the rules of a political election may have to be changed to make way for such a transparent system, blockchain is also ideal for informing business decisions, guiding general meetings, polling, censuses, and more.

The use cases for blockchain voting software are many and diverse. Its ability to engage and manage a constituency is crucial to the future of society, not just to produce a transparent outcome but to encourage all people to participate in their communities. The technology is still in its infancy but maturing alongside the young voters. It will one day help and be a crucial part of our collective future.

Chapter 11: Conclusion

What Does the Future Have to Offer Crypto?

Many people are left wondering what is ahead for all forms of cryptocurrency. Over just over a decade, it has exploded in popularity and functionality and made so much money for many people. Still, cryptocurrency remains in its adolescent phase and still has much room to grow. It feels as though, despite its repeated appearances in so many headlines, many people are still in the dark about cryptocurrency, and it has yet to break through the mainstream. What is next for cryptocurrency? Will it rival the dollar? Will Bitcoin break through the $70,000 value mark? Will cryptocurrency find its way into some major retailers? And if it does, what happens then?

Let's discuss the chance of crypto being used in big, established businesses and stores because, if that happens, cryptocurrency's popularity - and value - will grow by a whole lot in a short time. Since you are now an investor in cryptocurrency, this will significantly affect you in some incredible ways. But is it even possible? Will it happen?

What about Amazon? Is crypto headed toward Amazon? That's unlikely, to put it gently. Amazon is a behemoth of a company, the world's largest retailer. You would think it would soon adopt cryptocurrency and Bitcoin and allow users to buy their products with cryptocurrency.

You would be wrong. Amazon has never accepted any crypto and doesn't have any plans to. In 2014, the shopping giant said it hadn't gotten into the crypto game because it didn't see a demand from customers to use it. Since then, speculation has reigned about Amazon using Bitcoin in the future. However, the assumption has been largely unfounded because Amazon has made few moves to suggest it would warm to the idea any time soon.

Why won't Amazon accept Bitcoin? There are multiple rumors. One of the largest ones is that Amazon founder Jeff Bezos doesn't like cryptocurrency. He is a mighty man, one of the richest on Earth, and there is a good chance he isn't fond of a new currency that isn't the one that made him so successful. He may prefer regular, cold, hard cash like many wealthy citizens. The newspaper he owns, The Washington Post, published a critical piece about Bitcoin in 2016. Its title was "R.I.P. Bitcoin. It's Time To Move On." Many people saw that as a sign that Bezos was actively working against the growth of all forms of crypto.

But there are other reasons why Amazon may be shying away from crypto. Some speculate that Amazon isn't fond of crypto because it is too volatile. That is a legitimate reason to be wary of it. The value of crypto fluctuates wildly, much more than the dollar does. How would Amazon and its third-party online retailers price their products for Bitcoin when the worth of Bitcoin is all over the map? If the Bitcoin market settled down for a year or so, you might see Amazon begin using it.

Amazon has many behind-the-scenes deals with major credit card companies like Visa and Mastercard. Both major brands are not fond of Bitcoin and how it is shaking up the monetary business. To make the credit cards happy, Amazon may not accept Bitcoin until all parties can get along. However, it will be a long time before companies like American Express and others warm to Bitcoin because they are seen as a direct competition that is coming to change the status quo.

Perhaps another reason Amazon isn't using Bitcoin is that it is contemplating creating its cryptocurrency exclusive to the site. That would not be a surprising move at all. It wouldn't even be that original of an action. There are other eCommerce sites much more minor than Amazon that created their forms of crypto. These currencies are growing in popularity and can only be used in the areas they are designed for. If Amazon were to introduce its line of crypto, it would be a huge success and could even rival Bitcoin. That would be a significant reason why they are slow to accept it, because they may someday be doing direct competition against it.

It seems unlikely that Amazon will ever accept Bitcoin as a form of payment on their site. That is unfortunate and a massive blow to the crypto community. If a business as huge and ubiquitous decided to embrace crypto, it would be seen as a significant success story and make Bitcoin's popularity skyrocket seemingly overnight. Amazon holds the keys to making crypto and Bitcoin far more successful, but they aren't doing anything to promote its growth among average shoppers.

How Blockchain Will Revolutionize Everyone's Lives

Far too many people think of blockchain as the way to get Bitcoin or cryptocurrency. And far too many *more* people don't think about blockchain at all.

That's a shame because, in the years ahead, there is a perfect chance that blockchain truly will revolutionize the world and the lives of everyone you know. It might have changed your life already. You might not even know it yet.

What blockchain does is decentralize a system? It only focuses some data in one spot but sorts it and spreads it across a vast network. This network is always self-checking, updating, and tending to itself. It is always accurate and nearly impossible to infiltrate and disrupt or hack.

It is best to think of blockchain as a living and breathing creature, a creation that exists on its own and is self-sufficient and always stronger and safer than nearly any alternative.

Looking at it that way, you can see why blockchain can take the world by storm. From automobile creation to shipping and production of products to healthcare companies and even voting in local elections, blockchain can make everything run better, faster, safer, and more independently and efficiently.

Blockchain takes the pressure off the workers and puts it on a system and infrastructure that can withstand a lot. There are drawbacks to the blockchain, just like there are drawbacks to any approach, but it is safe, and it is almost always reliable.

More companies and businesses need to see the value and potential of blockchain. It has already founds its way into so many major players in the world, but there is so much more room to grow. If it does take hold even more, you can expect to see so much of your life perform better. There are many practical ways blockchain can be adapted to the everyday world, but many have yet to be discovered.

Blockchain is here to stay. It has allowed cryptocurrency to grow and blossom, and it will ultimately change so many other things. Blockchain *does* have the power to revolutionize your life and the world around you. It already has. And it's only just begun.

Thank You

You could have picked from hundreds of other books, but you bought mine, and I appreciate it. Thank you so much for purchasing my book.

Not that you enjoyed (I hope) my book, can I ask you for a tiny favor? Can you please post a review on the platform? You posting a review is the best way to support the work of independent authors like me. Your feedback will help me keep writing the books that will help you get the desired results. It means a lot to me to hear from you.

I am happy for anyone to reach out to me for help, comments, collaboration ideas, or feedback at brian@brianscottfitzgerald.com

My   Author   page   on   Amazon   at https://www.amazon.com/author/brianscottfitzgerald

Printed in Dunstable, United Kingdom

67775527R00119